Praise for *Your Child's Po*

"So many of the expectations we have for children, both at home and at school, are simply not in line with their natural development. This book will help shift your lens toward realistic ideas about what children are capable of, no matter their neurotype. If you are already familiar with Dr. Ross Greene's model (Collaborative & Proactive Solutions), you'll recognize Kelsie's neuro-affirming approach and appreciate how it inspires empathy for the child while also holding space for the adult experience. If you're just beginning this journey, you'll appreciate the specific behavioral examples, straightforward advice, and accessible format. And no matter where you are starting from, you can benefit from how the recommended strategies balance everyone's needs."

– Autball, Autistic advocate and educator

"*That child* is a phrase I have often heard, both as a teacher and parent. Sometimes it has referred to one of my children that has not behaved in the way that school has wanted them to. I know how it feels to have one of those children that teachers don't like. This is why I celebrate this book by Kelsie Olds, offering a ray of hope to parents like me. It would have been fantastic to have had a book like this when my children were young: to look up why my autistic/ADHD child behaved the way they did when they were younger, and to feel less alone in trying to work out what to do. More importantly, I would have placed this book in the hands of every educator that took care of my children. As a pedagogical consultant and teacher trainer, I know that there are many teachers who seek and need help with understanding children's points of view when those views do not align with what the school/society expects. The book is filled with non-judgmental suggestions as to what could actually be going on for that child, in order for adults to avoid knee-jerk reactions that make things worse. I highly recommend taking the time to not only read the book, but to have it close by to use when in need of Kelsie's wisdom."

– Suzanne Axelsson, play advocate and author of *The Original Learning Approach*

"In *Your Child's Point of View*, author Kelsie Olds, 'The Occuplaytional Therapist,' tells us how important it is to consider a child's point of view, lived experiences, and individual differences when raising and working with developing humans. I highly recommend this book for parents and educators. I love that the book provides a brain- and nervous system-based understanding of child development at every stage. I especially enjoyed the 'At School' chapter and agree with Kelsie that we must focus more on human connection and unstructured play in our schools. The book provides many actionable ideas for 'things to try' at home and in the classroom. It will make a positive difference in how you see and support the children in your life."

– Guy Stephens, Executive Director of Alliance Against Seclusion and Restraint

"Few things compare to the anguish of seeing your child suffer, yet feeling unable to make it better no matter what you do or how hard you try. All of us who have been there know it's not for a lack of devotion, determination, or effort: we love unendingly, advocate tirelessly, and negotiate hopefully. When that doesn't work, we cajole, beg, and probably yell a little. (Or a lot.) As a longtime family therapist and mom of four adult daughters, I own an embarrassing number of parenting books, and I have both taught and attended countless parenting courses. Too often, we find the same ideas repackaged with a slightly different spin, sporting little more than a fresh title. Or we see parenting recommendations and think, 'that might work for someone else's kid, but it would never work for mine'—which is almost immediately followed by feelings of frustration, hopelessness, and inadequacy. *This book is categorically different.*

Whether your child is neurodivergent or neurotypical, whether they are a toddler or a teenager, and whether you have parented for three years or thirty, this book is a gold mine of ideas presented in an incredibly user-friendly, compassionate, and nonjudgmental way—and in a format that is not only easy for exhausted parents to absorb and process, but will make you feel like Kelsie Olds is sitting next to you on your sofa watching daily life with *your* kids unfold.

One of the most powerful takeaways for me, which permeates the entire book, is that what our children are doing genuinely makes sense to them. Their efforts to communicate—no matter how confusing, stressful, or frustrating—are their attempts to tell us what they need. They are doing their best. And this book, in a profoundly simple way, gives us the wisdom, support, and guidance to do our best as well."

– Suzi Mohn, M.A., Licensed Individual, Couple, and Family Therapist

"Put this book at the top of your To Read list! As readers of 'The Occuplaytional Therapist' know, Kelsie Olds has an unusual gift: sharing about neurodiversity-affirming parenting in a relatable, practical way. You will see your kids and yourself in the examples—and walk away with fresh perspective on supporting both. Highly recommend."

– Cass Griffin Bennett, Autistic parent and AAC advocate

Your Child's Point of View

Your Child's Point of View

Understanding the Reasons Kids Do Unreasonable Things

Kelsie Olds, "The Occuplaytional Therapist"

ISBN: 979-8-3219-3488-3

Cover design by Courtney Herwicz.
Editing by Kristina Hawley.

www.occuplaytional.com

For Josh, who has steadfastly supported me in every project I've ever jumped into.

Table of Contents

Introduction

This is a book for everyone.

Did you read that sentence and still wonder if it includes you? I will be more specific.

This is a book for parents, first and foremost. The first three sections of this book help parents understand and empathize with what their children do, say, and think. I am a parent too; my two children are five and six years old now. My role as their mom informs everything I write. I am also parenting my children in a different way than I myself was parented, with the increased generational scrutiny and family tension that come along with that choice. This is a book for parents who are trying to do things a new way, for people who need someone to support them while they support their child. This is a book for biological parents, foster and adoptive parents (that's me!), single parents, co-parents, stepparents, and grandparents. Families are made in many ways, and all of them are included here.

This is also a book for teachers, therapists, coaches, mentors, tutors, youth leaders, principals, and **anyone who works with, cares for, or loves children.** The fourth section of this book focuses on understanding children at school. By trade, I am an occupational therapist who works with children. I spend a lot of my time explaining the progression of child development, including phases that most children go through, and what types of behaviors may indicate that a child needs more specialized support. This book gives lots of important facts about children's development and suggests strategies to solve some common problems that adults and children may have.

This is a book for anyone who ever was a child, **especially people who felt misunderstood as children.** It is for anyone who wonders why they react to things the way they do, and it may help explain their reasons to the misunderstood child living inside of them. The fifth section of this book is for reflecting on your own self as a child, understanding that child, and empathizing with them, too.

This is also a book for anyone who is a child right now. They might or might not actually like to read it, but it is nonetheless for them too. If a child were to do so, they might think, "This all sounds very obvious," because parts of this book explain child logic in a child's voice, or at least my best attempt at one. I chose to write those parts that way because I have noticed that many adults have forgotten what child logic sounds like—and because children have never been adults, they don't know how to adapt their language in order to communicate effectively with adults.

My hope is that this book will act like a bridge between the big humans and the small humans. I have worked very hard to consider all voices while writing it. The big humans are not always in the wrong for not understanding the small ones; the small humans are not always in the wrong for being misunderstood. Everybody is working together to try to get everybody's needs met. Sometimes that kind of teamwork can be hard, and sometimes a book like this one can help.

With all that said, I should admit one thing. I said this book is for everyone, but I need you to be willing to believe me when I say that **hurting kids—emotionally, physically, or mentally—does not make anything better.** For you, for your child, or for anyone. So, if you're looking for a book to tell you how to punish, discipline, embarrass, isolate, shame, or otherwise hurt your kid into changing something about themselves, you won't find that here. There are unfortunately too many books like that out there already.

Here, we're a team and we're working together; we're all humans and we're empathizing with one another; and we're accepting all the feelings that are part of the human experience.

It's okay if these ideas are new to you, and you're open to learning more. It's okay if this wasn't how you were raised, and you're changing things for yourself at the same time as you change them for your family. It's okay if you try really hard, and you still don't always get it right. That makes both of us, you and me, and the truth is that there's far more than just two of us feeling this way.

There are biological parents, foster parents, stepparents, and grandparents; teachers, principals, coaches, and tutors; aunties, uncles, caregivers, social workers, therapists, and counselors; and so, so many more of us who are all on the same side here, the one that says:

"We're on the kid's side.

A big human doesn't get more care, consideration, or respect than a small human just because they're big.

A tall human doesn't get their needs met at the expense of a short human just because they're tall.

Neither does an old human have to lose sight of who they are, or martyr themself on behalf of their young humans, just because they're old.

There is a way for all of us to be a team, and sometimes it's tricky to figure out what that should look like. Both these things are true at the same time, so we will do our best, feel the way we feel, and be kind to ourselves as we do."

This is a book for everyone.

If you flip through the book looking for a situation that sounds exactly like what you're struggling with, you may find faster answers. Its content is sorted by age, which may help narrow your search.

If you start at the beginning and read it all the way through instead, you will probably read about some things that are not directly relevant to you. You may read passages that remind you of worries you had at a different time in your life, and it may make you smile to realize how far you've come. You will probably also read some things that feel very relevant to you. Hopefully, **you will even start to pick up on the overarching framework of ideas that can help you find new ways to approach problem-solving.**

At the end of the book, you will find an appendix that explains in greater depth some of the more specialized terms that I sometimes use. Where possible, I provide brief explanations in context, but there are so many more complex thoughts I want to share about some of the nuances of child development and sensory processing. So, the appendix is there if you want more details, and then there is a bibliography to give you even more resources.

This is a book for everyone, and **I'm so glad that you found it.** We are changing the world together—the way we heal our own old wounds, and the way we safeguard today's children against bearing the same scars. I want you to be a part of creating that change. I want you to be included in giving and receiving that healing. **Welcome home.**

Babies & Toddlers

(0–3ish)

the adult's point of view

He doesn't listen to me. I try to only give him
directions when I need to for his safety, but he still
doesn't listen.

Whatever you're saying out there doesn't stick in my brain.
My own internal voice is TOO DISTRACTING, and what
you said a few minutes ago is already gone!

one possible child's point of view

Things to know...

- **The ability to reliably follow verbal directions is built on lots of smaller skills.** Children must comprehend the directions, store them in their working memory, plan how to move their body in order to follow the directions, carry out that movement plan, and control any other impulses that arise instead. Many of these skills don't emerge until age five or older.[1]

- **Auditory processing occurs on multiple levels.** People can hear noise, but not pay attention to it. People can pay attention to the sound they're hearing, but not comprehend it. People can comprehend what they hear, but not obey it. Knowing this can help you figure out what the problem is. Did your child hear and pay attention to you, but not understand your directions? Did they not "tune in" to you in the first place? Are they simply listening to their own inner voice instead of obeying?

- Immediate obedience is a fear response. **Children who are not afraid of their adults do not obey them instantly.** Sometimes their thoughts take a moment to catch up to what you're saying, or they want to negotiate, or they outright disagree with what you want them to do. That's why obedience isn't a realistic goal—instead, the goal is whatever you need to see happen (such as for your child to get dressed or stay safe from a hazard). There are many tools available to help the two of you reach that goal: playfulness, collaboration, negotiation, suggestion, support, verbal help, physical help, etc. Using these tools often takes longer, but protects the relationship between you and your child instead of relying on making them afraid.

Things to try...

- **Physically assist your child** with what you are asking them to do. Your child may be able to understand you better now than they could in infancy, but that does not mean they need any less help now than they did then.

- **As the adult, take full responsibility for keeping children safe.** When walking in the road, hold your child's hand, put them in a carrier, push them in a stroller, etc. Don't expect your young child to be responsible for their own safety yet. They may not be happy about this, which is okay. They are allowed to feel how they feel; you don't have to talk them out of their feelings.

- **Set up the environment for success.** Young children need lots of free play in environments that are safe for them to explore. This also minimizes the number of rules they need to listen to!

- **Make instructions playful when you can.** One research study found that children who were told to "pretend to be a statue" were able to follow directions for much longer than those who were told to "stand still."[2] Playfulness engages the child's brain in their native language of play and meets them at their cognitive level.

- **Keep instructions brief.** Toddlers can typically follow only short requests like, "Get your socks!"[3]

the adult's point of view

The moment my child finishes their meal, they shove their plate off their high chair and onto the floor. It's like a game to them. Suddenly, with no warning, there's food everywhere.

… OH, HEY, I'M READY TO BE DONE RIGHT THIS SECOND! Wow. I'm as surprised as you are! I'm learning to notice when my body is full, but right now, that feeling still sneaks up on me.

one possible child's point of view

Things to know...

- **Remember your toddler is not throwing food to intentionally annoy you.** It's easy to take young children's behavior personally, especially when we spend all day, every day with them—but the truth is that they don't think about how their actions will impact their adults until they get much older.
- **The skill of impulse control takes a long time to develop,** and the first leap in its development doesn't happen until a child is three to five years old.[4] When a child is younger than that, and an impulse enters their head (like "I'm done, get it away!"), they're going to follow that impulse. Their brain will not have the capacity to consider other, more logical measures until it physically matures. (See the Executive Functioning section of the appendix for more details about how impulse control develops.)

Things to try...

- **Watch your child's behavior for clues.** This may be easiest to do during their snack times and when you aren't focused on eating your own food. Your child probably has subtle cues that indicate they're done, such as eating more slowly, exploring the food with their hands, looking around, or wiggling.
- **Try to block your child** *before* **they throw their food.** It takes energy for a brain to come up with a new action plan and carry it out. To save energy, our brains like to repeat action plans that worked in the past. While we can't parent impulse control into a young toddler, we can redirect their brain. This interrupts their current action plan and begins to teach their brain a new action plan to follow. When the toddler picks up food and you can tell they're going to throw it, physically block their hand with your hand. Take the food and put it back on the plate if you think they're still hungry, or simply remove it and let them be done if you think they were communicating that they're done. This helps them build a new action plan.
- **Give your child examples of what to say.** If they can't speak reliably yet, say what you think they may be thinking, or what you would want them to say if they could. "Oh, you're all done with your food! Let's get it out of the way because you're all done." While you speak, you can also model the baby sign language for *all done*, as they may mimic a gesture sooner than they are able to say the words.
- **Use dishes with suction cups that stick to the table or high chair tray.** Even if your child figures out how to loosen the suction cups, using these dishes could buy you some time to block your child from throwing their food when they're done. You can also place food directly on the (clean) high chair tray or table in front of your child, instead of putting it all on a plate.
- **Talk out loud about your own body and feelings of fullness.** "I think I'm all done with this food. My belly feels full and heavy. I don't need to eat any more. I'm all done!" This gives your child's brain the language to conceptualize the sensations they are experiencing.

the adult's point of view

Whenever my child is upset, they scream. The volume and pitch of their screams are intolerable, and everyone else in the house is feeling frayed.

I had a feeling in my body that was HUGE and LOUD and UNCOMFORTABLE! When I scream, I feel all kinds of strong sensations in my body that make me feel a little bit better. My screaming must help my grown-ups understand how I feel, because it seems like now they feel bad, too!

one possible child's point of view

Things to know...

- **Toddlers can't reliably take the perspective of another person.** Toddlers are egocentric: they perceive the world from only their own point of view. Sometime between five and nine years old, children start being able to accurately take the perspective of someone else, as a result of repeatedly practicing interactions with adults and peers.[5] A younger child isn't screaming to annoy you on purpose—they just can't perceive how it will feel for you.
- **Young children experiment with volume** as part of the process of learning how to communicate.
- Yelling or screaming provides a lot of sensory feedback to the body: it vibrates the throat, pushes air hard through the abdomen, and stretches the jaw. **This strong sensory feedback releases some of the tension in the body, which makes the body feel more settled afterward.** Does that mean yelling is a perfect solution to frustration? Of course not! But it helps to know that it makes sense for people to yell when they're mad, and it takes time and maturity for them to learn other coping mechanisms.

Things to try...

- **Try to react as if your child had said "Help me, please" or "Ouch, that hurt" instead of screaming, and verbalize these thoughts for them aloud.** Model what you think they are feeling in words so the next time they want to express the same concept, they have a script they can try.
- **Play "loud/quiet" games at other times**—not when your child is upset, but when the two of you are playing. Experiment with whispers and shouts, and narrate what you're doing. "I'm using my whisper voice like a tiny quiet mouse. NOW I'M USING MY LOUD VOICE like a great big lion!"
- **Wear earplugs, play music, or choose another strategy that helps you cope with overwhelming sounds.** This could even help both of you in the long run. If your child ever struggles with tolerating noise or chaos when they get older, they will have already seen you model using coping strategies to get through that.
- **Focus on keeping yourself regulated.** Your child will grow out of this stage and learn other ways to verbalize their feelings, even if you never correct them. Instead, explore which coping strategies help *you* feel more settled and supported. Try taking deep breaths, checking your body for tension, or running cold water over your hands to help keep you in a calm headspace, even when your child is upset. Then you can help them solve problems as a wise adult partner, instead of colliding as two dysregulated people lost in their emotions.

My toddler *has* to learn how to use the toilet or else she will be kicked out of day care.

I'm not ready to use the toilet yet. My body needs to figure some things out first, and it needs more time for that. I'm still little, and no amount of practicing or rewards can make my body ready to do things it's not capable of yet.

one possible child's point of view

Things to know…

- **You cannot control what comes out of a child.** You can facilitate a child's access to a toilet and even decide when the child should sit on the toilet, but you can't control what comes out of the child. Children who resent being intensely controlled—whether in regard to toileting or in another area of their lives—will often assert their own power by refusing to use the toilet, or by peeing and pooping in places other than the toilet.
- There are three factors that, taken together, indicate a person is ready to use the toilet: **physical readiness, interoceptive readiness, and emotional readiness.** Physical readiness involves moving to and balancing on the toilet, managing clothes, wiping, and flushing. Interoceptive readiness requires being able to interpret the bodily urge to go. (Interoception is explained in more detail in the appendix.) Emotional readiness includes being willing to stop playing, being willing to "let go" of a part of their body in the process of toileting, and managing developmentally normal feelings of fear or anxiety around toileting. A child can be ready for one or two parts of the process but not yet ready for all three.
- **Culture does not dictate children's development.** Just because a teacher, grandparent, friend, book, or person on the internet thinks your child "ought to be ready by now" does not necessarily mean that they are.

Things to try…

- **Wait to teach toileting until your child is ready.** Most children aren't quite ready at three, but become so between ages four and five, if they are not pressured by an adult to learn earlier. (Most children also show a mild surge of interest around age two, but this interest often fades. Two-year-olds are also often not ready in one or more of the three ways described above.)
- **Alternatively, begin to teach toileting on your preferred timeline, as long as you do so** with the understanding that your child will likely not be fully independent. It will take much more involvement on your part to support them interoceptively, physically, and/or emotionally. For example, you may need to interpret their body's cues (holding self, "potty dance") for them if their interoception isn't ready yet. This can lead to feelings of failure or frustration for the adult or the child. If that happens, **it's best to continue using diapers until everyone feels confident and "no pressure" about it.**
- **Trust children to learn "different rules for different places."** If your only reason for toilet training is because of school or day care rules, know that many children can successfully toilet only at school and still use a diaper at home. This does not confuse them or make them less likely to learn once all three factors are in place.

She keeps lying to us. It's a real problem. Nobody is going to get mad at her; nobody is threatening her; we just need to know the truth.

Why are you asking me this? Don't you already know the answer? I thought we all knew exactly the same things!

one possible child's point of view

Things to know…

- **Three-year-olds are only barely beginning to understand the concepts of reality and fantasy.**[6] They are not intentionally fabricating events, as their brains haven't even pinpointed what fabricated events are yet. Imagination, wishes, and memories all blend together when a toddler tells a story.
- In many ways, **honesty is a social construct.** A child may be trying to gauge from your question if you want to know what really happened or if you want to feel happy. Toddlers know they would much rather feel happy than sad, so they usually tell you whatever they think will make you happy.
- **Children begin to develop the knowledge that other people see, think, and know different things than them sometime between three and five years old.**[7] Your toddler may literally not understand yet that you don't already know exactly what they know.

Things to try…

- **When you are feeling frustrated about a child being an unreliable witness, imagine they are an actual baby,** only a few months old and unable to speak. Regardless of what they had witnessed, you wouldn't expect them to tell you about it. It's the same with toddlers, even if it seems like they "should" be able to tell you.
- **Set kids up for success.** Don't ask questions that you already know the answer to in the hope that they'll practice telling the truth—for example, "Did you brush your teeth?" when you already know they didn't. That type of questioning can confuse kids, who may assume you already know and then try to guess what you want to hear.
- **Be aware of your own use of sarcasm, jokes, and teasing.** Your child may be emulating the types of things they've heard you say, depending on how often these types of playful lying are used in your family.
- **Label the ways people play with language.** Introduce terms like *joking* or *tricking you* when you're already being playful with your child. For example, if you're playing with their toy farm animals, make the cow say "meow," followed by, "hey, cows don't meow! I'm just joking." If your child lies down with a blanket and pretends to sleep, you could say, "Are you tricking me?"

He has to stop spitting! He spits when he's angry, and when he's not. He holds mouthfuls of water and spits at the dinner table. It's disgusting and upsetting.

What happens when I put things into my body and take them back out? What happens when I hold water in my mouth and then let go of it? What if I push it out? I love experimenting!

one possible child's point of view

12

Things to know...

- **Schema play is a normal type of exploration in the toddler years.** Schemas can be thought of as phases of play that children go through. Container play—in which children put things in various types of containers, pour from one container to another, spill, and so on—often overlaps with a fascination with spitting. In a way, mouths are containers too!
- **It is okay to ignore the behavior.** Most likely, the phase will pass on its own. If you aren't feeling resentful, and there are no genuine hygiene concerns, this is often a successful option.
- **Alternatively, it is okay to set a limit.** You will have to help enforce it. Your child cannot simply follow verbal directions; they need you to be their impulse control, since this skill has not developed for them yet.
- **This is another example of how adults can't control what comes out of a child.** Children instinctually realize this and often experiment with what they can get to come out of their body (words, saliva, food, urine/feces) when they are looking to regain control over their lives.

Things to try...

- **Spit in the sink, tub, or backyard.** Tell kids where they CAN spit, and redirect them there if you're choosing to hold a limit. Or go all out and lean into the science of it—when my own kids went through this phase, I bought unsweetened Kool-Aid packets, mixed them into cups of water I set up in our backyard, and had the kids swig and spit with multiple flavors and colors. Turning it into a fun activity with a designated place and time takes the power struggle out of it.
- **Wordlessly offer a wipe or towel** with a calm, non-shaming demeanor. Sometimes kids will happily take it and wipe up the mess. If they do a less-than-ideal job, try to wait until they're distracted with something else to do a more hygienic job (if you'd like), so they feel responsibility and ownership over their own cleanup.
- **Observe your child to see if there is a precursor or inciting event that is causing them to spit.** For example, spitting because they're feeling bored versus spitting because they just drank too much water would merit different solutions.
- **Spend as much time outdoors as you can!** It's typically much less of a problem to spit in the grass than it is to spit on the couch.

My child won't eat unless the food is taken from *my* plate or she's seen me already eat some of it.

I'm not just a baby who puts anything and everything into my mouth anymore; I am more careful about what I put in my mouth now. I know you're pretty smart, so if you eat it, it's probably okay for me to eat too!

one possible child's point of view

Things to know...

- **It's developmentally normal for toddlers to become increasingly cautious about what goes into their mouths** as they grow out of the baby stage.[8] As children become more mobile, they have more access to potentially dangerous things. To keep them safe, their sensory system matures: their hands and fingers become their primary sensory exploration organs, not their mouths.
- **Letting your child eat food off your plate is okay** if it's working for your family and you're not feeling resentful. (That last part is applicable to nearly everything in parenting!)
- **Holding a limit around your child eating food off your plate is okay** if it's right for you and you do not respond to your child harshly or in frustration.

Things to try...

- Knowing that this is a developmentally normal phase, **decide whether this is important to you.** Some people feel strongly about their own body, space, or belongings being left alone, food included. (I am one of them.) Other people are unbothered by sharing their food.
- **Give your child the opportunity to serve food onto their own plate.** Even a very young toddler can use serving utensils with support, or move finger foods from a communal plate onto their own plate.
- **Serve at least one food that your child likes with every meal.** That way, they know there is something safe and reliable available. For many children, fruit, rice, or bread work well for this purpose.
- **Do not force children to eat.** Except in rare medical circumstances where a doctor or healthcare team is already involved, children should always have the option not to eat at a particular meal. (It may also help to know that many toddlers and children prefer to eat more earlier in the day, and less or nothing at all in the evening, which may differ from how their adults eat.)
- **Serve meals at predictable times** so your child knows that if they don't feel they can eat right now, there will be a predictable meal or snack in two to three hours they can wait for.
- It may help with general nutritional worries to **conceptualize your child's eating habits over the course of a week,** rather than a day. Some children eat a truly varied diet each day, while others may eat plenty of protein and no fruit one day, then eat only fruit and no protein the next day!

He has a medical condition, and to manage it, his doctor has ordered us to put ointment on his skin every day. We try to make it quick and give him choices. We *have* to do it… I just wish he would stop fighting it.

I NEED to fight this. You get to decide what to do to me? Well, *I* get to decide how I feel, and I don't like it! Since you aren't stopping, fighting is the only way I can tell you how strongly I feel!

one possible child's point of view

Things to know...

- Adults often want to teach very young children about body rules and consent. This is important and admirable. It can get muddled, though, because **young children do not truly have 100% bodily autonomy.** They need adults to make decisions about their health and safety.
- **Your young toddler needs a confident leader who accepts their feelings—that's you—more than they need complete bodily autonomy.** Otherwise, you end up with a standoff in which the adult *must* do something for their child's safety, but feels they can't do it without the child's consent. Then the child must either mask their emotions or experience a health crisis, neither of which is helpful.
- Adults often try to rush through uncomfortable things. **Some children, especially young children, actually prefer to slow down.** It feels counterintuitive to adults, who think, "Let's just get this unpleasant thing over with and move on." But for children, rushing through an unpleasant thing may feel like a sensory whirlwind, which they then struggle to process. Going slowly, even while uncomfortable, helps them understand and make sense of what is happening to them.

Things to try...

- **Role-play doing the uncomfortable thing**—put pretend (invisible) ointment on a teddy bear; pretend your toddler is a doctor giving you a shot. Talk through your role-play. Use it as an opportunity to explain what happens during the uncomfortable thing or to play-act out experiencing the emotions your child experiences.
- **Give meaningful choices, and reduce choices that your child doesn't find meaningful.** Having to make decisions during something hard, sad, or scary can be empowering, but it can also be exhausting. Your child may want to decide which arm to get the shot in, or maybe they just want to cry and not be asked questions. Either way is okay.
- **Offer a distraction.** There are times in life when feeling our emotions all the way through is really important. There are other times when we just have to suck it up and do something that isn't fun. Listening to music, eating a snack, watching a show, listening to a podcast, playing with a toy, or using other distractions can help with those not-fun-but-necessary things. Keep in mind, though, that while distractions may make it easier to get through the challenging moment, those emotions will probably come back out later—and that's healthy.

the adult's point of view

She's such a Daddy's girl. Mom's feelings are hurt, Dad
is exhausted, and the list of things she won't allow
Mom to do just gets longer and longer.

I LOVE hanging out with Dad. I can never get enough of
the things I love the most, that make me feel the best, and
right now, hanging out with Dad makes me happier than
anything else.

one possible child's point of view

Things to know…

- It is extremely common for toddlers to have a preferred parent. **Toddlerhood is a time of strong opinions, black-and-white thinking, and blunt, simple language skills.** "Want Dad!" or "No Mom!" fit all three of those criteria.
- **It's not our children's job to allow us to do things.** Most of the time, when adults say, "They won't let me…" they really mean, "They get upset when…" Remember that it's okay for children to be upset, with a supportive and loving adult nearby. In this example, it is absolutely okay for the child to prefer Dad for bathtime, for Dad to be unavailable for bathtime, for Mom to do bathtime instead of Dad, and for the child to dislike this plan. **Nobody is doing anything wrong.** The child feels their emotions, the preferred parent steps away and trusts the non-preferred parent to be a safe adult, and the non-preferred parent reminds themself that this is a normal developmental phase and they don't need to take their child's feelings personally.
- Sometimes it doesn't work out that way, and the non-preferred parent can't keep themself regulated or avoid taking their child's feelings personally. If that happens once or twice, it usually means the adult is very tapped out that day. If it happens chronically, it could be a sign that the adult needs to address something in their own heart, their own mind, their own past. Either way, **the onus is on the adult to get themself the help they need** so they can be a safe person for their child.

Things to try…

- **Be predictable when possible.** That could mean the adults switch off who does bathtime and bedtime every other day. It could mean that for a time, the preferred parent does a particularly challenging activity with the child to make it easier for everybody, and the non-preferred parent steps in somewhere less emotionally fraught. Whatever pattern works for your family unit, having one the child can anticipate often helps.
- **Reframe what your child is saying in your own head.** I was the non-preferred parent in my family. When it started to hurt my feelings, **I would pretend my son was saying, "Dad is so great. I love Dad," instead of saying, "Go away Mom, I don't want Mom."** I would respond as if he was too, with something like, "I know you love Dad so much," instead of saying, "You're making Mommy sad."

Dropping my child off at day care has somehow spiraled out of control. He sobs and clings to me. I try to remind him of all the lovely things he gets to do there every day. He's so excited to go until he gets there.

I know you wish I could always have a good day and only feel comfortable, happy feelings. But in my heart, I'm feeling both excited to go and sad about missing you! I just love you so much, I want to play with my friends AND stay with you. Can I have more than one kind of feeling at once and still be okay?

one possible child's point of view

Things to know...

- **Separation anxiety often has two peaks in childhood,** around eight to nine months old and again between fifteen and eighteen months old.[2] When children begin to learn about object permanence—the concept that something continues to exist even when it's out of sight—they also realize for the first time that their beloved grown-ups are continuing to exist somewhere without them!
- Sometimes parents feel concerned because their child seems to suddenly be more anxious about separating from them, even at familiar places. While it's always wise to investigate if you have reason for concern, **your child's anxiety doesn't necessarily mean that something bad has happened.** Children move into and out of phases of clinginess as their brains grow, mature, and figure out new things.
- **Children often take cues from their adults.** If the adult seems distressed about separating from them when they are sad, the child will feel more distressed. If the adult seems empathetic but unworried, it gives the child the freedom to express their feelings without internalizing new worries.
- **It is okay for children to feel sad.** Feeling sad about a big transition, like separating from a beloved family member for hours, is normal. You don't have to try to coax your child out of it or persuade them to feel a different way.

Things to try...

- **Honor your child's emotions by acknowledging them, instead of trying to talk them out of their feelings.** You can say empathetically, "I know. It's so hard to say goodbye," or, "I'm going to miss you too, baby," without having to add a negation to your statement like, "... but you'll have so much fun!" (Sometimes when we negate our children's expression of the biggest emotion they're experiencing, they instinctually believe they must express it even harder for us to *get* it.)
- **Make up a shared goodbye ritual.** This could be a special handshake, fist bump, or hug; a little phrase you say or song you sing every day; or something as simple as giving your child three kisses because they're three.
- **Talk about times when you feel more than one emotion.** At other times—not during drop-off, when your child is already upset—talk about your own conflicting emotions. You could say something like, "I feel happy to go see my friends at work, and sad because I am going to miss you. I feel two feelings at the same time."

She's picking up bad behaviors from other kids at preschool, like hitting and spitting. We try to talk about listening to the adults, not to other kids, but it doesn't seem to help. She's a good kid, she just follows bad influences.

I learn way better from other people my own age than from whatever the grown-ups say. Sometimes when they talk, all I hear is, "blah-blah-blah." Now, this seemed to work for my friend, so let's find out if it works for me!

one possible child's point of view

Things to know...

- **Some children really do "try on" things they see their peers doing.** This is a normal way for humans, who are very social beings, to learn. Seeing someone else's body do an action, and then trying to mimic it with your own body, is an important skill.

- Sometimes, especially in young childhood, **similarly aged children move into and out of the same phases.** For example, almost every toddler goes through a throwing phase of some kind. (It's called the *trajectory schema* and is one of the ways our brains learn about the laws of physics.[10] See the appendix for more in-depth information about schema play.) So, occasionally, adults may mistakenly attribute two children going through the same phase at the same time as one child copying the other.

- Schools and day cares often expect parents to talk to their children at home about something that is happening at school. But **young children live in the moment to a much greater degree than most adults.** During the day at preschool, they are not thinking about what they talked about with their parent last night, in a different building, in a different context... they're thinking about the present moment. Lecturing children about behavior hours after it happened is usually ineffective at best, and stressful for them at worst.

Things to try...

- **Play games of "school/day care" with your child** in which you pretend to be the child (or that a stuffed animal is the child), and your child is the teacher. You may be surprised what they share about their days!

- **When your child tries to hit you, gently block their hand.** If your child is persistently hitting other kids, you know that your child needs support to interact with their peers for the time being. **They need you close by,** sharing your impulse control and your regulation with them, because their nervous system can't provide those things independently yet. This is also true at preschool. Toddlers hit other toddlers, and they need adults close by to help be their impulse control.

- **Make sure your child knows that they can tell an adult when other children hit, push, or spit at them, and remind yourself that it's a normal part of toddler interactions.** The child who hits is not a "bad child", or even behaving badly. They just need adults to support them while they are so small. (Your child might be the instigator sometimes, too!)

the adult's point of view

She hits the dog and sometimes even kicks him. We tell her "gentle hands" and she repeats it, but then continues to play way too roughly with him.

This creature is the most complicated and interesting toy we have. I can play with him in all sorts of ways. I don't know what it means yet to be alive or to have empathy… I'm just exploring! What happens if I do this?

one possible child's point of view

Things to know...

- **Around this age, it's extremely common for children to be unable to play safely with a pet without close supervision.** They developmentally can't understand yet that the pet is alive or that living things feel feelings, let alone guess what those feelings may be. They are still learning to read human nonverbal cues and body language, such as tone of voice, facial expression, and so on; they are even further from being able to accurately interpret *animal* nonverbal cues and body language. Even when it is obvious to an adult that a pet is distressed, the child is both unaware of the pet's distress and developmentally unable to put themselves into the pet's frame of mind to understand that they don't like this type of play.
- To put it simply: **your child may think, "If I'm having fun, everyone is having fun!"** and be unable to visualize that another participant in the interaction, whether human or animal, feels differently.
- Some children may lash out at a pet when they are angry. It can be really hard to see it this way, but **this is a form of effective communication**—your child is very angry, and they are sharing their anger with you by making you angry too. That doesn't mean you should let them harm your pet. However, keep in mind that your child is doing a great job of sharing with you how they feel, which can help you remember what they really want: to be heard and understood.

Things to try...

- **Keep your child and your pet separated** when you can't be close by to help keep everybody safe. Some suggestions: your pet stays in a specific room that is off-limits to your child; you put the pet outdoors; you use a pet/baby gate; you stay with your child in a closed room; you go outdoors with your child for most of the day; etc. You can focus on separating either the pet or the child.
- **Play "gentle/rough" games in other contexts** that have nothing to do with your pet. Introduce these concepts to your child through play. This could include you and your child pretending to be animals, roughhousing, or playing with stuffed animals. If your child has a beloved stuffed animal, model being gentle with it, petting it, and talking kindly to it.
- When you are available to moderate interactions between your child and pet, **block your child's hands or feet if they are going to hit or kick the pet.** Make sure your pet has an escape route in case they get uncomfortable. Remove your child or pet from the situation if it gets too chaotic—not with a punitive mindset, but to keep everybody safe. Try to watch for early signs of your child getting too excited or wound up, and intervene. Doing this helps them interrupt their brain's action plan that ends in aggression toward the pet and helps them build a new one (as discussed in more depth in the Motor Planning section of the appendix).

My gifted, spirited child talks literally nonstop and wants me to answer every question. When I explain that I need to work for a little while or that I'm tired of answering questions, she cries, whines, and hits me.

Yes, I'm smart and advanced in some areas… but my heart and feelings are still little! I've only been alive for a short while. Long enough to know I adore you, but not long enough to have friendships or other social connections. I just want to do what makes me feel good, and that's spending time with you.

one possible child's point of view

Things to know...

- **It's not our children's job to meet our needs.** This can be really frustrating sometimes, especially when the reason feels legitimate to the adult, like needing to work. But it's still not the job of a three-year-old to meet the needs of their parent. Instead, the parent must make arrangements to meet their own needs. (If that's truly impossible, such as in an emergency where childcare is unavailable, the parent must accept that everybody will need more support and energy than usual, and things will still likely go poorly.)
- **Children mature in different ways and on different timelines.** A child can be very verbal and still emotionally immature, just like another child can be very physically capable but not have many words yet.

Things to try...

- **Try out various chores or hobbies, and invite your child to do them with you** whenever possible. This gives you new topics to talk about, engages your brain, and introduces your child to a new skill or interest!
- **Make time for yourself to socialize with other adults.** Lots of tools exist to help you stay connected. Can you text a friend throughout the day, call somebody after bedtime, use social media in ways that create authentic connections, or meet up with someone you love on weekends? Support needs look different for different people, but if you can find what feels good to you, doing it regularly can dramatically improve your well-being.
- **Recognize when you are your child's entire support system.** Just as desperately as you want to socialize with other adults, your young child wants to socialize with you—possibly even more so, because while you may have many avenues for support and friendship, they *only* have the connected caregivers in their life for everything from casual conversation to co-regulation. You can empathetically understand their strong feelings here, because you have very similar feelings!
- If you have loved ones or relatives who wouldn't mind doing a FaceTime or Zoom call with a babbling toddler, **set up your child to chat away with someone who can happily listen** to buy yourself at least a few minutes to do something else. (It doesn't even matter if they're intelligible, as long as the adult on the other end of the call can nod, reflect, and say "ooh" and "ahh.")
- **Consider how adults converse with your child most of the day.** Do adults typically ask them lots of questions? Oftentimes, well-meaning adults don't know how to talk to a child, so they ask them questions like, "What sound does this animal make?" or "What color is this?" in an attempt to bond. In turn, this can make the child believe that the best way to bond with people is to ask them nonstop questions. If this is true of your child, try to introduce new types of conversations for a while, and see if that helps. You can try simply commenting on something you're thinking about, explaining a scientific fact, or sharing a memory.

Key themes from these years:

1. Your child feeling sad does not mean you are doing something wrong, or that you need to fix something. Your child feeling sad is not inherently bad. **Human beings just feel sad sometimes,** your child included. Your role is to be present with your child in their feelings, whatever those feelings are.

2. Overall, adults tend to talk far too much at children. Sometimes adults mistakenly believe that if they can just explain everything rationally, it will mean something to a toddler. **Lengthy verbal explanations are not helpful at this age.** Adults may remember feeling confused, left out, or misunderstood as a child, so they try to compensate by giving their two-year-old oral paragraphs of information. Alternately, some adults do this in an effort to avoid brief but "harsh" communication, like snapping "no" or "stop" at their child all day long. These are both noble pursuits, but they still don't make toddlers receptive to long rambles. The child's brain can't process all those words!

3. This age is exhausting, emotionally and physically. Being exhausted all the time does not mean you are doing something wrong; it simply means that this age is exhausting. That is because **toddlers are exhausting.**

4. Adults often erroneously take intellect, social skills, or early language abilities to mean that a child's brain can accomplish complex emotional or executive functioning skills, such as obeying verbal directions promptly, managing their impulses, or remembering to follow directions given to them a long time ago. **Three-year-olds are not any less three, just because they are good at talking.** These children are still babies in many ways.

5. Sometimes the responsibility ends up falling on a child for adult problems. "The school is being unreasonable, so my child has to change." "My co-parent is being unreasonable, so my child has to change." Unfortunately, the world is a crummy place sometimes. We can't remove all the obstacles or control all the moving parts. **And it's still not the two-year-old's fault.** If there is a problem to solve, the adults need to come up with a way to solve it —and, sometimes, the only remaining option that doesn't push a child to do things they aren't ready for yet is to accept an imperfect situation.

6. **Language is still so new to children at this age** (yes, even if they talked early!). They are not reliable storytellers who use only literal, factual language. To young children, words are still like a big, clumsy tool to whack stuff with and see what happens. Taking their clunky language personally is unhelpful and probably a sign that you're exhausted. Expecting their language to be wholly rooted in reality is asking way too much.

Notes

[1]Engle, Carullo, and Collins, "Individual Differences."

[2]Ivanova, "Development of Voluntary Behavior."

[3]CDC, "Important Milestones."

[4]Best and Miller, "A Developmental Perspective."

[5]Rubin, "Egocentrism in Childhood."

[6]Sharon and Woolley, "Do Monsters Dream?"

[7]Milligan, Astington, and Dack, "Language and Theory."

[8]Cole et al., "Correlates of Picky Eating."

[9]Jummani and Shatkin, "Pharmacological Interventions."

[10]Louis et al., *Understanding Schemas*.

Littles & Middles

(4–8ish)

My child constantly asks questions they already know the answer to. If I say, "In five minutes, we're going to go get in the car," they'll say, "Who, me?" Who else would I be talking to?

I'm still thinking about what you just told me, and need a few more seconds to process the words. I know how to buy myself a little time: if I ask you a question, it'll slow down this rushed conversation so I can think.

Things to know...

- **Children often use questioning in a different way than adults do.** They may ask questions they know the answers to for many reasons: to reassure anxiety, check whether they have the correct information, practice predicting what someone's answer will be, make conversation, or clarify information.
- Children also may not really be asking a question to get an answer at all, but simply be **buying themselves time to process and formulate an appropriate response.** Especially if their processing speed is slower than the time it takes for their adults to get impatient, they may have learned that it's better for them to say *something*—anything at all—than nothing, while their brain processes what was just said.

Things to try...

- **When your child asks a question they obviously know the answer to, or asks a question like "What?" reflexively, try simply pausing and waiting for a couple of seconds.** Their brain may catch up to the conversation and answer its own question. If not, you've modeled how sometimes people need a couple of seconds before they can answer a question, which is also good for your child to see.
- **Make sure you actually have your child's attention before you begin talking to them.** Sometimes calling their name first, or touching them on the shoulder gently, can cue their brain to begin attending to what you're about to say. Otherwise, the second or two it takes for their brain to transition is a second or two of your sentence that's lost.
- If you have the patience to do so, **it's okay to just answer the questions,** even if they are annoying or you think your child probably already knows the answers.
- Phrases like "asked and answered" are sometimes suggested in cases like this, but those can be very abrupt and clearly communicate to the child that they're being brushed off. Instead, consider asking something more authentic and less snappy, like **"We just talked about that—do you remember what I said?"** This approach can help the child think back to the past and guide them in remembering, which can be a challenging skill.

the adult's point of view

He has no time for me during the day, but once it's bedtime, he has a million questions that must be answered immediately.

Going to bed means saying goodbye to my favorite person in the world and being alone for a long time. The quiet space makes room for my mind to think about all kinds of new things that I was too distracted to contemplate earlier. Maybe if I ask one more question, it'll make you stay just a little longer...

one possible child's point of view

Things to know...

- **Many children feel most comfortable sharing their thoughts right before bedtime.** This can be hard for adults, who may be looking forward to some quiet time to themselves. Anticipating this pattern can help a little, when the adult can reserve energy for answering bedtime questions instead of being surprised by them.
- There is no "right" age at which children can fall asleep independently, or right way to handle bedtime. **If something works for your family, and everyone's needs are being met, it's okay to keep doing it.** If your current bedtime routine doesn't work for your family, which can happen when someone is feeling resentful or unsupported, there are lots of strategies you can try. (These could include room-sharing, lying with your child until they fall asleep, siblings sharing a room, a pet staying in the room, changing the room's lighting, playing music or white noise, and so on.)
- **Some families do better with a "bedroom time," after which the child plays or reads quietly in their room until they fall asleep, than a bedtime.** Maybe this could work for you, too.

Things to try...

- Some children have a hard time simply lying in silence and darkness, waiting for sleep to come. **Listening to music, a sleep podcast, an audiobook, white noise, or a guided meditation may help.**
- Some children worry that if they don't share their thoughts right away, they will forget them. It could be appropriate to **let your child keep a notepad by their bed to write their thoughts down on, or a small voice recorder.** (For other children, these would be too distracting—you know your child best.)
- **Get your child ready for bed earlier** to make time for more talking, if needed.
- In our modern and busy world, kids don't often have opportunities to think silently, other than when they go to sleep. **Notice whether your child has any other time of day when they can choose to simply think,** and if they don't, consider how you could make opportunities for that. Spending time outdoors, such as going for a walk, can work for this. Offering companionable silence at a time when you would usually ask questions helps create space for your child to think, too.
- If your child has a hard time with you leaving the room, but you want to move toward them falling asleep more independently, **make a plan to check in with them every five minutes,** then every ten minutes, and so on. That way, they'll know you're predictably coming back, and the transition to being alone doesn't feel so scary.

She refuses to take responsibility for anything. When I point out something that needs to be fixed, she says, "That's not my fault," or even tries to blame ME!

Oh no… I made a mistake. The shame and embarrassment I feel are too much to deal with, so I'm hiding those emotions behind anger. If you fight with me about my anger, that gives me something new to be angry about and I can keep up the protective pretense.

Things to know...

- **Perfectionism is a normal phase for many children.** It is especially typical around age six, which is the stage of middle childhood when the fear of failure and desire to be the best are strongest.[1] It makes sense: the brain has developed to a point where it can imagine creating amazing masterpieces or completing tasks perfectly, but not to a point where it can actually carry out those things consistently. How frustrating!
- **Anger is often, but not always, a secondary emotion.** Anger protects and defends us. Feeling angry usually feels safer than being vulnerable enough to feel sad, scared, hurt, or embarrassed. When children suddenly get angry, they may be protecting themselves from another, scarier emotion.

Things to try...

- **Avoid the blame game when you can.** "Your shoes are in the kitchen again; will you put them where they belong?" may trigger a rush of shame in some children, whereas "Can you put your shoes away? They're in the kitchen" may not. One shows frustration, while the other is a more straightforward request.
- Some kids respond best to indirect communication, like simply saying, "Hey, there are shoes in the kitchen!" Other kids do better with humor, like saying in a silly voice, "Hey, I'm not cooking shoes for dinner! These don't go in the kitchen!" **Experiment with what kinds of phrasing feel the most authentic to you and work the best for your child.** Also, remember that as your child matures, **the types of communication that feel best to them may change.** What felt silly and delightful at five years old may feel condescending at seven.
- Keep in mind how often your child is corrected each day. Depending on how many different groups of adults they're around, it may be quite frequent. Whenever you can, **let go of the small, unimportant things,** like when your child is doing something inefficiently or strangely but is not having trouble nor asking for your help.
- Being aware of how your child usually picks fights can help you **avoid getting sucked into arguments.** If your child tries to blame you for something absurd, they probably already know it's absurd. You don't have to argue about it. Alternatively, this is another opportunity for humor, depending on your child's personality. You may be able to lean into their accusation in a silly (but not mocking) way: "I made you spill that milk from all the way over here? My mind-powers must be a little off today, I was trying to make you give me a hug!"

My daughter whines that she's bored and needs something to do, but then she refuses every game or play suggestion that I make!

Boredom scares me. I can tell the adults don't like it either— they fill so much of their bored time with electronics. Maybe if I keep pestering them, they'll figure out a magical answer to solve all my boredom. I haven't found it yet, but it has to exist. My adults know more than me… I bet they can solve this.

one possible child's point of view

Things to know...

- **Children often use the word *bored* to mean a variety of other things.** Boredom is a nebulous emotion. Sometimes children use this label when they're really feeling anxious, antsy, lonely, or something else.

- As they get older, **many children try out nuanced social skills, such as hinting that they want something** without saying so outright. "I'm bored" can be a key hinting phrase, like when the child is hoping the parent will allow something special: for example, an extra hour of tablet time, or to go to the neighborhood park or pool. The child may be trying to use sophisticated language or avoid the painful rejection of an outright "no." These types of hints can be frustrating for both the adult and child, because the conversation seems to be about one thing but is really about another.

- Remember that **allowing all feelings includes accepting your child's boredom and annoyance.** It's okay for your child to feel this way and for you to not solve it for them. You can even let them know that you trust them to solve this problem.

Things to try...

- **Consider what underlying feelings may be present.** If your child is awaiting a birthday party happening tomorrow, they may be feeling excited and eager for the day to be over. If your child is worn out and it's half an hour before bedtime, they may be exhausted and seeking connection with you. **Let your ideas about their underlying feelings guide your suggestions for your child, and talk specifically about those ideas with your child.** "I wonder if you're bored because your brain really wants it to be tomorrow. If I get out the colored paper, would you like to make some last-minute party decorations?" is a very different solution than "I think you may be feeling all tired out. Shall we snuggle on the couch and read a book together until bedtime?"

- **Name the subtext** if you believe your child is hinting at something (e.g., asking for more screen time). You can try prompting, "Is there something you're hoping to ask me?" or answering more directly, like "We're not going to do more screen time today, but I can help you brainstorm other ideas if you want."

- **Collaborate with your child to come up with ideas, and write them down** to give them more gravitas. You could brainstorm with your child about what they would like to do, invite their solutions, and take notes. Having the solutions written down makes them feel more serious and grown-up.

He only has one speed: GO. He runs, jumps, and flips all over the house constantly. During these loud and chaotic exercises, he frequently knocks things over and annoys other family members. It's so frustrating.

My body knows what it needs to grow and develop. I need to move, I need to flip, I need to jump. I'm not trying to annoy anybody; I'm just doing what I can feel that my body needs.

one possible child's point of view

Things to know...

- **Children need far more whole-body and outdoor play than most modern lifestyles allow for.** This is a really tricky thing about society. Unfortunately, healthy development does not naturally follow or even fit into the typical restrictions of today's world. At the very least, being aware that children typically need three hours of outdoor play every single day can help their adults understand *why* they're so rambunctious when they're stuck inside.[2]
- **One particular type of sensation, called *proprioception*, is often the most regulating type of sensory input.** In a nutshell, proprioception is your sense of awareness of your body in space. Children who are moving their bodies all over the place are trying very hard to get this whole-body, regulating sensory input. They know that they need it to feel at home in their bodies. People can get proprioceptive input from activities that involve exertion, impact, or pressure. (There is a Proprioception section in the appendix that provides further details.)

Things to try...

- **A child who tends to run, lift things, and climb on things may be looking for lots of exertion.** Playing games or giving them chores that involve heavy physical work (like pushing a vacuum or pulling the garbage bins to the curb) may help them meet that need, and could even contribute to a sense of helpfulness.
- **Children who tend to get "aggressive" and wrestle, hit, or jump on couches or beds may be looking for lots of impact.** Playing games or offering activities that involve heavy physical impact (like punching a punching bag, jumping on a trampoline, or crashing into a pile of pillows) may help them meet that need.
- **If your child tends to drape themself over furniture or other people, and/or squeeze into tight spaces, they may be looking for lots of pressure.** Putting heavy blankets on your child, giving them lots of big bear hugs, or having them crawl underneath a pile of cushions or a beanbag may help them meet that need.
- **Take the whole family outside, especially in natural environments, as much as you can.** The natural world offers a lot of sensory input, proprioceptive and otherwise, that is very regulating.

My child makes constant noise. Sometimes it feels like it's just to annoy me.

My brain works better with just the right level of noise in the room. If a sound is bothering me, I can make my own to cover up the one I don't like. If there's nothing interesting to listen to, I'm content to make my own sounds.

one possible child's point of view

Things to know...

- **Your child is not making constant noise to annoy or frustrate you on purpose.** When people feel sensitive to a form of sensory input, like noise, too much of it can start to feel like a personal attack. But just because your nervous system feels threatened, does not mean that your child intended to be a threat.
- Children are frequently unaware that they're making noises with their mouth, humming, or tapping with their hands. **Making sounds to oneself is actually a very common sensory regulation strategy for all humans.**
  - If a person is feeling understimulated, they need more sensory input to feel comfortable or be attentive. **They may make noise to raise their level of sensory input.** Making that noise could provide more input in the form of sound in their ears, impact to their hands (like from clapping), vibration in their mouth (while humming), etc., depending on how they are creating the sound.
  - If a person is feeling overstimulated, they need to remove, escape from, or filter out something that's overwhelming or annoying. **They may make noise to cover up an irritating form of sensory input.** They are now in control of what they're hearing, and drowning out a bothersome sound.

Things to try...

- **Wear earplugs, wear earbuds that can play music, or play soft music in the room from a speaker**—some pleasant sound for your ears to latch on to, or to block out the annoying noises. Sometimes hearing music will also help your child filter out a noise that was bothering them, and they will stop making their own noises.
- **Talk out loud about your own sensory needs in a non-judgmental way.** The best way to do this will vary depending on your child's age. "My ears are a little tired, so I'm putting on my headphones" may work well for a four-year-old. "I love all the chaos, but the sound is overwhelming me. I'm going to go in my room and take a break" may work for an eight-year-old.
- **Consider giving your child unrestricted access to pleasant sound**—for example, making sure they have a music player they can listen to, or an instrument they can play with headphones on. It should be something they have full control of, while also considering the needs of everyone else in the home.

I *try* to validate my child's feelings! Let's say they're frustrated and throwing things. I'll say, "It's okay to be frustrated." Even as they are still throwing things, they will explode at me, "I'm NOT FRUSTRATED!"

You telling me how you thought I felt might have been helpful when I was still a baby who couldn't talk, but it is NOT helpful now! You are not inside my body. You DON'T know how I feel. I'm not the same person as you, so if you say I feel something, then I say: NO, I DON'T!

Things to know...

• **Narrating feelings can be helpful for young children, but as they get older, they may become annoyed by it.** As they start to understand how they differ from their parents, it begins to feel more and more irritating to have someone label their experience, especially if the label is different than the one they would've chosen.

• **Every human will encounter frustrating things at some point in their lifetime.** Children typically encounter child-sized problems and adults sometimes encounter adult-sized problems. Learning to navigate these and experience the frustration, rather than minimizing or ignoring it, is an important process.

Things to try...

• **Simply listen and don't say anything.** Sometimes our kids just want to be able to rant, rage, scream, or sigh, without needing any verbal input from us.

• If you need to talk, **describe what you see happening** instead of what you guess your child is feeling—for example, "Oh no, those two pieces aren't connecting," rather than, "Oh, you're getting frustrated."

• Sometimes children get more frustrated when their parents seem to be emotionlessly describing their experience, rather than truly feeling it. What you're saying may resonate more with your child if you **say it with a tone of voice that matches the emotion you think they are feeling:** "Oh man, you're FRUSTRATED!"

• **Model describing your own feelings out loud,** not only your child's. Children take more cues from our actions than from what we explicitly teach them.

• If you notice your child is becoming frustrated, **offer help before they get to their breaking point.** That's not always possible, since sometimes they will get frustrated when you're not looking, but if you hear warning signs— like grunts, groans, or an "Arrrgh!"—it may be worth asking, "Do you want help with that?"

• **Draw their attention to the warning signs, too.** Explaining how you came to the conclusion that your child was frustrated may help them understand their own body better, as well as where you're coming from. This can be done with or without labeling the specific emotion. "I see you squeezing your fists and I hear your voice getting shaky. Do you need help, or maybe to take a break?"

My child seems strangely possessive of the freedom to sing and dance. We'll see him doing something cute and join in, but then he will start yelling, "Only I can sing that!" It hurts our feelings, when all we wanted was to connect.

I didn't know you were watching me. I don't want to be perceived right now. I imagined this moment in a specific way, with myself lost in the music, not with you interrupting and making noise.

one possible child's point of view

Things to know...

- As babies and toddlers, children are unaware that others have different thoughts and perceptions than they do. **Then, as they get a little older, children begin to understand that other people *aren't* seeing through their eyes and thinking their thoughts.** Eventually, they realize that other people may be looking *at them* and thinking things *about them.* This can be an alarming or upsetting realization!

  - Imagine if you found out that someone else had put a secret camera in your home. You might feel indignation, rage, embarrassment, and shame about having your privacy invaded. **Many young children feel this way when they first realize their adults are watching them and thinking about them, especially when the child did not expect it**—and because they are young and immature, they didn't know yet to expect it—even when it seems obvious, like when they are in a public place or communal living room. It is from this emotional place that children react defensively to being watched.

- It is also developmentally normal for young children to seem very "controlling" or "demanding" when they insist on things being a certain way. They are emerging into a stage where they can anticipate the future and form a mental picture of how they expect something to go, and **they feel empowered to try to direct events as they unfold** in order to make them match their own mental picture. These are powerful skills to learn!

Things to try...

- Singing out loud can be very regulating for all humans, adults included. It makes sense for you to feel frustrated if your child is sensitive to you singing out loud. **Find a different time and place for this powerfully regulating activity** that won't bother your child—perhaps you can sing in the shower, in the car by yourself, or while you go for a walk.

- **Don't interrupt your child when they seem to be enjoying something privately,** even if the setting is public. As they grow and mature, they will discover how they can achieve true privacy; in the meantime, it's okay for them to enjoy their ability to be "in their own world" even when surrounded by other people.

- **Imagine that your child has the language and self-regulation skills to ask you more calmly.** If they were consistently able to say, "Actually, I was enjoying listening to my own voice; could you just let me sing this one solo, please?"... how would you react? Try reacting that same way to them now, with grace for the fact that they aren't mature enough to ask that way yet, but someday they will be.

I find it so boring to slow my pace to match my child's speed. They want to dress themself, but it takes forever. Plus, I have to remember to give them ten-minute and five-minute warnings for everything. It's so much mental load.

My whole body and brain are totally immersed in what I'm doing. Thanks for thinking about all the grown-up stuff for me, so I can keep thinking hard about my own work.

one possible child's point of view

Things to know…

- **Transitions are almost universally challenging.** Transitions are times when you move from one activity or location to another. Transitioning requires your brain to stop thinking its current thoughts, shift into a state of uncertainty, and move toward a new setting in some way. This can be tricky for adults, let alone for children, who often need much more support:
  - perhaps emotionally, in letting go of what they were doing before;
  - perhaps physically, to complete some element of the transition, like getting shoes on; or
  - perhaps executively, in determining what steps need to take place for the transition to happen. (More information on this third area, executive functioning, is available in the appendix.)
- Giving your child the opportunity to practice tasks independently when they're not frustrated, struggling, or asking for your help is massively important. **Remind yourself that you are doing an awesome job of parenting while you wait patiently** for them to catch that zipper or straighten that sock!

Things to try…

- Depending on a child's age and developmental level, describing things in minutes may be completely useless for them. **Measure time in terms that are personally relevant to your child:** for example, "We'll leave the park after you slide three more times," or "I'm going to play your favorite song on my phone, and when it's done, it's time to go get in the car!"
- If experiencing boredom, slowing down, or practicing mindfulness are challenging for you, **keep a fidget in your pocket** so you have something at hand to fill the inevitable small, unstructured moments of parenting. There are lots of those. It can help for your brain to have a plan, like "When they're not doing anything wrong, just taking a long time, I'll practice taking ten deep breaths" or "I'll spin my fidget ring around five times before saying 'Hurry up' again."
- In non-urgent situations, **choose a number and count to it in your head while you wait.** Counting to 100 while a child confidently works to buckle their own seat belt gives your brain a simple task to focus on, gives you a concrete end to the waiting period, and gives your child ample time to practice their new skill without being hurried by an impatient grown-up. (Plus, during the counting period, your mind may wander to something more interesting anyway.)
- Alternately, **listen to podcasts, audiobooks, or music on earbuds.** Any of these can help an adult struggling with their own feelings of understimulation while trying to be more patient.

My son is so destructive. He plays very roughly with both his toys and siblings. He takes everything apart, and so many things end up getting broken.

I NEED to take things apart to find out how they work! I need to run, and jump, and explore, and play! It's so hard to live in a world where everyone expects that I will be still and quiet. I want to know everything, explore everything, and do everything.

one possible child's point of view

Things to know...

- **The word *destructive* can mean a lot of different things.** Knowing which definition you are seeing play out in front of you can help you identify when your child needs extra support, and what that support could look like.
  - One parent may say their child is "destructive" when their child **needs a lot of movement** and incidentally knocks things over as they try to meet that need for movement.
  - Another parent may say that their child is "destructive" when their child **takes apart toys to figure out how they work** rather than playing with them in the expected way.
  - A third parent may say that their child is "destructive" when their child **plays with toys in a way that puts a lot of wear on them quickly.**

Things to try...

- **Play with recyclables, consumables, or cheap materials** that can be dismantled or destroyed and then discarded, guilt-free. Building forts out of cardboard and then tearing them apart through destructive play results in the same amount of still-recyclable cardboard that simply recycling the boxes in the first place would have!
- If you have a little engineer on your hands, **look for things that can be taken apart**—perhaps in local thrift shops or at garage sales. (There are even social media groups, such as the extensive Buy Nothing network, for giving things away.) Deconstructing old appliances; prying nails out of wood; snapping old, dried-out markers in half to find the ink pad inside... taking things apart like this is often the first step to learning how to build, construct, and invent new things.
- **Play outside as much as possible;** this gives growing bodies the chance to move and explore more freely. This also sharpens their internal sense of "where my body is in space," which needs to be in place for a child to grow out of clumsiness and accidentally knocking things over.[3]
- Sometimes children seem especially "destructive" when they are **instinctively trying to gain proprioceptive input.** Finding a substitute—such as lifting something heavy; giving tight, squeezy hugs; hanging from a bar; climbing a rope; or jumping, then crashing into a pile of pillows—may help channel that sensory need in a safer direction. (Proprioception is explored further in the appendix.)

the adult's point of view

If I say, "Stop poking your sister," she says, "I'm not poking, I'm tapping." Then, if I say to stop tapping, she'll switch to, "I'm not tapping, I'm kicking!" The pedantic arguments are so aggravating.

I am frustrated about how many things are out of my control, but my clever grasp on the nuances of language makes me feel powerful. It's fun to exercise my debate skills with my adults, too. If they wanted to be more specific, they could be more specific, right?

one possible child's point of view

Things to know...

- **Kids move into and out of phases of being very pedantic about language.**
  - One phase occurs around age four, once a child's vocabulary has expanded and **they have begun to understand that words can have many synonyms, as well as degrees of specificity.** They begin to practice their new words in context: should this be called a dog, or specifically a terrier? What makes a dish a *dish* but not a plate?
  - Another phase takes place as children begin to be able to think more abstractly, often around age seven or eight. **They begin understanding how to think about problems from different angles and perspectives.**
- For some children, this isn't a phase, but a pervasive personality trait. **These children often grow up to be adults who are intensely oriented toward the pursuit of truth and justice.** It feels important to them that what everyone says is actually true, complete, and accurate. That can be frustrating, the same way that many childish personality traits can sometimes be frustrating, but it's still important to honor.
- **There is no need to approach this childhood stage with fear.** Adults frequently imagine that their child will become a pedantic or unlikable adult if they let them flex their reasoning skills right now. That's not the case! Child development doesn't work that way.

Things to try...

- If your child effectively invites you to an argument, **ignore the invitation.** You don't have to engage in a discussion about the word choice at all. If your child says, "I'm not poking, I'm tapping," move closer to the siblings who are fighting and begin mediating without adding commentary: "So what's going on that's made everybody's so frustrated? What do you need right now?"
- Depending on your kid's personality, **defuse the pedantry with humor.** When your child says, "I'm not poking, I'm tapping," say in a playful voice, "Well, no poking, tapping, pinching, flipping, flopping, bleeping, snorping, or plarping either!"
- **Consider exploring more indirect language** if you feel that your directness toward your child could be contributing to or causing the arguments. For example, you could approach a fight between siblings by saying, "Hey, what's up?" and then hearing out both sides, rather than, "Stop poking your sister." **Being pedantic with language can be a child's attempt to regain power they feel they lack,** and children often feel disempowered when an adult talks down to or corrects them.

the adult's point of view

Whenever I tell him to do something, his knee-jerk reaction is to get frustrated with me. He can't just do what he wants 100% of the time!

I wish they could see that I was busy doing something and lost in my own thoughts! It's startling to be interrupted and annoying to be told what to do, especially when I don't even care about the thing I'm supposed to do. At least I know I can safely share how I'm feeling about it.

one possible child's point of view

Things to know…

- Starting in toddlerhood, all humans begin making predictions about what they expect to happen next. From these predictions come plans and expectations. These plans give brains the ability to prepare for the day (or hour, or even next few minutes). **When their plans are interrupted or canceled, some people naturally have a hard time with that—children included.**

- Human beings who live in close proximity to one another sometimes get frustrated with one another. If children never communicate frustration to their parents, it's usually not because they aren't ever frustrated, but because they don't feel safe communicating frustration to their parents. In a way, **your child's frustration is a sign that your child feels safe sharing their feelings with you.**

Things to try…

- Consider whether you are expecting your child to drop everything and obey a command immediately, or whether you are **communicating an expectation and allowing them to fit it into their plans.** Additionally, consider whether they *know* that it's the latter and not the former!

- Use language like "When you get a chance," "When you're done with that," or "When you get to a good stopping point…" to clearly **communicate that the two of you are partners in accomplishing what is needed,** rather than framing yourself as a superior handing down orders.

- Think about the locations where you find yourself regularly having to tell your child to do something. Can any of these interactions be "outsourced" to a visual cue or other reminder that your child is in charge of? Some examples are an alarm on a phone or tablet, a sign hanging in a bathroom, or a list posted in a communal family room. Sometimes, taking an extra step to **make sure the reminder comes from an object instead of a person** can make the reminder feel less like an attack.

- If you can **gain your child's attention and make a connection first,** it may help your child feel less like you only call their name when you want them to do something. You could gently touch them on the shoulder, comment positively on what you see them doing, or ask an earnest question about something they're engaged in.

She refuses to do simple things that she already knows how to do and insists she needs me to help her. She's known how to do them for years. She doesn't need my help.

Please take care of me, even though I am big. Don't expect me to do everything all by myself just because I physically can; I emotionally can't.

Things to know...

- **Kids often ask for help when they are really asking for connection.** Children may go through phases of greater neediness related to their own development, or in reaction to big changes like a new sibling being born, school expectations increasing, or a younger sibling learning to walk. These prompt children to reassess their roles in life. Some children may handle that by reaffirming that their role as your baby hasn't changed!

- **Children, like all people, have variable capacity from day to day, and sometimes even hour to hour.** A child may be exhausted by a day that required lots of self-control at school and social skills at home, and ask you to button their pajamas, even though they're capable of doing it themselves.

- Asking for assistance with something they already know how to do can help children process the eternal push-pull of growing up: **they become more mature and independent, but still want the security of being nurtured.** Language like "you're a big kid" or "you can do it by yourself" uses that dichotomy, which is often a child's greatest internal struggle, to try to motivate them to do something. But that struggle must be moved through at the child's pace, not manipulated by others. **When a caregiver can honor the child's expression of where they're at by lovingly meeting their needs, they reassure their child that they will always be taken care of**—that no matter how independent they get, they won't be alone.

Things to try...

- If you have the grace and ability to help your child with what they're asking for, then **help them!** Don't feel pressured to withhold help out of fear for the future, or to try to make them "act their age."

- If you are unable to help your child right away, like if you're busy or your hands are full, **verbalize the details of when and how you can help**—e.g., "I'd love to get that for you as soon as I…" or "I can help you after I put these things in the car." Finish with the gentle reminder: "… or you can do it right away if you need to." Let your child choose whether they need immediate results or connection more, and then honor their choice.

- If you're unable to help, **offer empathy.** "I'm sorry, buddy, I can't get that for you. I know it's frustrating."

- **Initiate playing "baby" at a different time.** Cuddle your child, talk in a baby voice, and fuss over them like you would a much younger child. Talk about their itty-bitty nose, eyes, fingers, and toes; wrap them up in a favorite blanket; maybe even help them drink from a water bottle as if it were a baby bottle!

- **Pull out baby pictures, or videos from when your child was a baby, and look at them together.** Talk about your favorite memories, especially if you can think of any you haven't told them about before.

She keeps threatening us. She'll say, "I'm going to hit you," or "I'm going to kick things," and then if we don't stop her, she'll start hitting and kicking.

Whoa—I have a whole new feeling in my brain. I can anticipate what my body is going to do before it actually does it. That's so different from before, when my body would just move and I had no warning about it. I'm so angry! I'm going to share this warning with my adults.

one possible child's point of view

Things to know...

- **Making threats is a sign of brain maturity.** To threaten, a person has to imagine what they might do and then transform the movement impulse into language, all while not following that impulse. This is a major skill!
- For some children, **threatening can actually be a form of asking for help.** When children begin to develop impulse control but don't have it fully in place yet, it can be frightening for them to be inside their mind as they realize they're *about* to hit but don't know how to stop it. It's like they're giving their adult a glimpse into their mind: "Please intervene! I'm not sure how to stop myself."
- Children may make realistic threats, such as "I'm going to hit you," or fantastical threats, such as "I'm going to cut you up and put you in a volcano!" These threats do not mean that your child is a sociopath. **Your child is using the strongest language they know how to use,** because they're feeling the strongest feeling their body knows how to feel, and they're trying to tell you about it.

Things to try...

- Sometimes adults react to threats with as much severity as they would react to the action itself taking place. For some adults, being told "I'm going to hit you" can make feelings like "How dare you disrespect me!" flare up just as strongly as if the child had actually hit them. **Try to reframe the threat as a warning in your mind,** as if your child were helpless or out of control—"Help, I'm about to hit you!"
- **Come up with a short script that feels authentic to you** and that you can reach for as a helpful response when this situation arises. With my family, I frequently say, "Do you need my help with something?" or "Okay, I can help you," while moving my body to block a hit or kick. Sometimes this means holding my child's hands; sometimes it means moving out of their range (or ushering a sibling out of their range) so there is no one left to hit or kick.
- For some children, **a warning of impending aggression can be a bid for sensory feedback, especially of the proprioceptive type.** If the situation allows for it, this could be a prime opportunity to start a pillow fight, grab somebody's leg and get into a wrestling match, or pull them in for a bear hug. (See the Proprioception section in the appendix for further details.)

My child tends toward pessimism. When we leave events at which he clearly had a wonderful time, he starts complaining right away.

I'm so disappointed that the fun thing is over, my disappointment colors everything. I need to process, like grief, how much it hurts to be done. Maybe focusing on the things I didn't like will make it easier to leave.

Things to know…

- Some people can clearly picture in their mind how they hope something will go. They may be able to visualize plans so well that any small deviation from that picture in their mind feels like a disappointment. These people often grow up to be wonderfully dedicated to whatever it is they love to do! They can work and work at a task they enjoy until their product perfectly matches the way they imagined it. **This often looks like pessimism or nitpicking in young children when it's still an immature, unrefined skill.**
- **Transitions are hard.** Moving from one thing to another is a challenging time. Leaving events usually means going from something fun to something unstructured, boring, or otherwise not-fun. It makes total sense that a child would feel unhappy in that moment and express their unhappiness, even if that means reflecting back with a negative lens on what just happened.

Things to try…

- **Listen empathetically to what your child has to say.** Don't rush to contradict them or immediately remind them of the fun they had.
- **Reframe your perception of their expression of unhappiness.** Imagine if they knew how to say: "I was having a great time, and I'm absolutely crushed that we have to leave. I just need some time to process and cry before I'm ready to remember the good times." You might personally feel differently, but you would likely respect their wishes.
- **Verbalize your own conflicting emotions.** For example:
  - "I loved it when we went down the slide together, but I definitely did not enjoy how hot and sticky it was outside. I'm looking forward to getting home where it's air-conditioned, even though I'll be sad to not be playing at the park anymore."
  - "I am so tired and low-energy after spending all day out—and having to leave now makes me feel even worse, because it was so much fun. But I'm happy that I'll always have memories of riding those rollercoasters with you. I'm sad and happy at the same time."
- **Take pictures or video during exciting and delightful events.** These will help you remember the delight that took place during the fun and may someday spark discussion or even nostalgia with your child, once enough time has passed that they can look back on the day's events fondly.

The older sibling keeps telling the younger sibling to do naughty things that they're not supposed to do.

Ooh, I knew I could play with toys or play with my body, but I've only just learned how to play "with" somebody else like they're a toy. If I use the right words, I can get them to do things. This feels so powerful, sophisticated, and grown-up—I want to explore it more!

Things to know...

- **It is normal for children to play around with social dynamics as they get older.** This type of social experimentation and play can take many forms: arguing, joking, tricking, manipulating, lying, threatening, insulting... these are all alarming to adults, but exploring them is a natural part of learning how language works and the power that it can hold. (That doesn't mean the adults have to let it play out without interfering, but it does mean that the adults don't need to panic when their child experiments like this.)
- The other side of the coin—the younger sibling misbehaving as directed—is normal too. **It is normal for children to experiment with cooperating with what someone tells them,** along with rebelling against what someone tells them. It's also normal for them to happily take someone else's directions as an excuse to misbehave. In and of itself, it doesn't mean anything long-term about their susceptibility to peer pressure or the life choices they will make.

Things to try...

- **Sidestep the argument about who is at fault and focus on setting limits instead.** If snacks are being taken out of the pantry and eaten inappropriately, then enact a limit around the pantry, the snacks, their accessibility, or the kids' supervision. Don't get dragged into an argument over whether it's the older or the younger sibling's fault. **You can use passive, rather than active, language to sidestep the blame game:** "I notice the shampoo is getting squirted into the sink, so I will put it away for now." Or simply introduce the new limit without saying anything at all about the events that prompted it. Different strategies are appropriate for different ages.
- **The older sibling may be looking for control.** Can you find other ways to help them feel powerful? **Play games that put your child in the position of power**—e.g., the person who pauses the music for freeze-dancing, or the person who gives the instructions in Simon Says. Look for areas of responsibility they might like to claim but aren't currently allowed to—perhaps you pack their snack for school every day, and they'd like to try doing it for themself.
- **The younger sibling may be looking for connection.** Can you set up ways for the siblings to connect meaningfully? **Invite them both to do a fun activity together,** or introduce something new that connects to an interest they share.

Key themes from these years:

1. **You do not need to jump a decade down the road with your worries.** Your child doing something annoying or inconsiderate now does not mean that they will be an annoying or inconsiderate adult. They are supposed to be immature and childish. They are not mature. They are children!

2. **Children still use language in a lot of non-literal ways around these ages.** They have a wider range of vocabulary available to them, but they don't yet have the years of experience with social nuances, connotations, and other subtleties that adults have attained. They reach for the biggest, strongest words they know when they have big, strong feelings. They experiment with crude, offensive, shocking, surprising, humorous, and boundary-pushing language. They make mistakes and miscalculations. All these things are part of the refinement process that leads children to be able to confidently express themselves throughout the rest of their life!

3. **Even as your kids get older, they are still very young.** They have been alive in the world for only a few years. They have had a grasp of language for even less than that. They have met a few people, seen a few places, and developed a few patterns of behavior. They don't have extensive experience. Don't expect them to be grown up!

4. If you didn't have the opportunity to parent your child from birth, or you initially parented in a more controlling way, you might find yourself struggling more in this phase, since you have less physical control over what your child does than you did when they were younger. It's harder to shift gears and start collaborating with your child later in life, but it's not at all impossible.[4] No matter what you and your child have been through, you haven't "messed them up" or "ruined them." **There is still so much of their childhood left, and this is the perfect time to start approaching life with a teamwork lens.**

5. This is the age when it starts to become apparent that you can't control everything in your child's life. In both their social life and at school, **they begin moving in spheres that don't include you as much.** Letting go of this control is hard—and it's important practice for both of you. Let your child try things; let them fail at trying things; support them empathetically while they figure those things out; believe that they can figure it out. Let them see you believing in them, too.

6. This was true in the baby years, and still is: your child feeling sad does not mean you are doing something wrong, or that you need to fix it. Your child feeling sad is not inherently bad. **Human beings just feel sad sometimes,** your child included. Your role is to be present with your child in their feelings, whatever those feelings are.

Notes

[1]Ames and Ilg, *Your Six-Year-Old.*
[2]Hanscom, *Balanced and Barefoot.*
[3]Hanscom.
[4]Greene, *Raising Human Beings.*

Tweens & Teens

(9+)

My child will go absurdly far to avoid admitting they made a mistake. They'll even turn it into something to blame me for.

Anger feels more tolerable in my body than humiliation or shame. If I can make it your fault somehow, then I can be justifiably angry… and then if you respond with anger, I feel even MORE justified in my own anger.

one possible child's point of view

68

Things to know...

- **Tweens and teens are going through a lot of changes to their understanding of morality, authority, and power structures.** They can undergo a complete shift every two to three years![1] The childish, black-and-white world in which "good people choose to do good things, and bad people choose to do bad things" is fading away. In its place are more nuanced, complicated perspectives: people behave in all kinds of ways, for all kinds of reasons; people can have good intentions and still end up with bad results.
- **Teenagers may hold themselves to impossibly high standards,** whether or not the adults in their life have actually expected that level of perfection out of them. They may feel that they ought to have grown out of making mistakes (or certain types of mistakes—e.g., physical clumsiness or forgetfulness) by now. The overwhelming emotional ups and downs of puberty magnify the feelings of crushing embarrassment or disappointment in themselves if they do make a mistake—**and you're a safe person for them to lash out at.**

Things to try...

- Drop your need to be right, or for your rightness to be acknowledged. This is easier said than done, and it takes inner work for the adult. **Ask yourself what you're afraid will happen** if your child says, "I didn't mess it up, you did!" and you simply say "Hmm," or "Oh," or even nothing at all.
  - Some adults fear that their child will grow up to be irresponsible or always blame others. It may help to understand that **learning how to sit with the uncomfortable emotions of having been the one in the wrong, or who made a mistake, takes experience and practice.** Every time the child practices, they will get a little better at it—but if the child tries to pick a fight and the adult shows up to fight them, the child will sidestep the emotional practice and instead feel justified in their anger toward the adult.
  - For other adults, it simply feels intolerable to be blamed for something they didn't do, and **they react to false blame as if it's a threat to their own safety.** If this description resonates for you, your emotional reaction to being unfairly blamed probably has more to do with pain in your heart or from your past than with the child in front of you. It takes work, but is worthwhile to try to separate those feelings out.
- **Defuse the situation with humor or playful sarcasm.** Robin Einzig wrote a lovely blog post on joking with her teenage daughter about how *everything* is her fault, even things that couldn't conceivably be her fault.[2] The child knows that logically that's not true; the adult knows the child knows; and saying it anyway is an easy way to convey, "We're in this together, you and me, versus this annoying, inconvenient, and frustrating world."

He literally announced to us, "I'm a procrastinator now."
He waits until the last second for everything—to get ready
for school, to get his homework done… it's stressing
me out!

My brain isn't motivated to do the thing that's expected of
me. I figured out a weird trick, though: I can use my fear of
failure to fuel me instead, as long as I wait until close
enough to the deadline that working on it feels like an
exhilarating rush!

one possible child's point of view

Things to know…

- **Dopamine is a chemical in the brain that makes it possible to initiate an action.** The brain creates dopamine for various reasons; one of those reasons is that the brain is interested in something.[3] If a person has to try to do something they are not interested in, their brain won't make dopamine (unless it finds some other reason to do so), and they literally can't start taking that action.[4]
- **Brains can also initiate actions when sensing a threat.** The threat of running out of time to complete a task before a deadline is one that people commonly seek out, whether consciously or unconsciously, to motivate themselves to do something. (There's more information about action planning, also referred to as motor planning, in the appendix.)

Things to try…

- **Work together to discover the reasons behind the things we have to do.** Discuss, for example, why homework is important or why morning hygiene tasks matter. Avoid catastrophizing, and be sure to **connect to what's actually meaningful to your child.** "If you don't do your homework, you'll never graduate and get a job" may feel like an out-of-touch exaggeration, but "Practicing your writing will help you create even better scripts for your YouTube videos" may actually connect with a child's own personal goals.
- **Tell your child about how brains make motivation.** Acknowledge that what they're doing is clever, even if it's not sustainable long-term. Talk about ways to make their tasks more interesting or delightful, or about other supports that will help their brain become comfortable enough to get motivated—for example, eating an enjoyable snack while doing homework, or listening to their favorite music while doing their bedtime routine.
- If excitement or competition feel like good "fuel," **consider how you could turn a required task into an exciting competition:** for example, by recording how long it takes to complete the task, and racing against others or to beat your own best time. This strategy could work for you or your teen.
- **Check out apps that gamify required tasks** to make them more fun and enjoyable, such as Habitica, Finch, or Forest. Try out one of these alongside your child, and see if it helps with missing motivation.

She's much too old to be crying, flailing, and throwing herself down when she doesn't get what she wants.

I really do think of myself as an adult, at least most of the time. But when things are falling apart in my life, my whole brain falls apart too. I want to scream, "I don't know how to deal with this! Stop expecting so much from me!" My disappointment and sadness drown me like waves.

one possible child's point of view

Things to know...

- **Emotions are ageless and genderless.** There is no age at which humans outgrow feeling sadness. The common, yet false, expectation that we do is disproportionately applied to boys across many cultures. Be mindful of the messages you send your children about whether and how they can feel their feelings.
- **Sometimes children who have felt unheard in the past feel that they have to turn their emotions all the way up to maximum in order to be validated.** If something happens that they dislike, and they just frown about it, they're expected to carry on anyway, but if they fall apart sobbing, someone will at least comfort them first. If a child's emotions consistently go unheard at "level one," they might feel like they have to turn them up to "level ten" every time.
- **It's really hard for developing brains to cope with the overwhelming hormonal changes that happen during these years.** Disproportionate waves of sadness can catch anyone, of any age, by surprise sometimes. During puberty, kids are even more susceptible to becoming emotionally overloaded by circumstances that might have caused only minor disappointment otherwise.

Things to try...

- **Speak about your own range of emotions that fall under the umbrella of *sadness* so that your child learns that language.** For example:
    - "I feel so disappointed, this did not turn out how I wanted it to."
    - "I'm exhausted from the long day we've had, and it's making my emotions feel very sensitive."
    - "I was looking forward to that event so much and then it got canceled—now I feel devastated."
- **Consider whether your approach with your child has been validating or indifferent.** For example, if you're reminding your child to take the trash out, and your attitude is brusque and impatient ("Just get it over with! It'll take ten seconds, why are you making this into such a big deal?"), your child may feel like they have to make it a big deal to show you how they feel about it. Instead, if you approach them with validation ("Hey, I know this sucks. We're all doing things that aren't fun to take care of our family. I know you're unhappy, and I really appreciate the help"), **their inner narrative may shift because they feel seen and understood.**
- At a quiet and cozy time, **look at your child's baby pictures together.** Talk about memories from when your child was little. Think together about all the ways in which they have grown, touching on both the things you treasured from their younger years and the things you enjoy about them now as a big kid. Give your child a dedicated time to feel little, cared for, and beloved without having to do anything to earn it.

I have to return to my child over and over to wake them up in the morning. If we set an alarm, they'll ignore it or hit snooze fifteen times. They just won't get out of bed.

My brain is legitimately not awake. *I* am not awake. All my logic, my lovely relationship with you, my care and concern about you, and anything else that might make me want to cooperate… all of that is still asleep, too.

one possible child's point of view

Things to know…

- **As their body reaches puberty, a teenager's natural sleep cycle shifts.** They continue to need as many hours of sleep as they did when they were younger, but their body naturally produces sleep hormones later in the evening than it did before.[5] Though some individual teenagers do prefer waking up early, most teenagers' circadian rhythms shift so they become "night owls" as they go through puberty—with the side effect that they're much drowsier in the mornings.[6]
- Many adults prefer to snooze their alarms before waking up, or have other bedtime and morning rituals of their own. **Your child's preference may just be part of the normal range of human preferences.** On the other hand, your child's preference may also be just a phase; you don't have to worry about what their future could hold if they don't learn to wake up easily now. A teenager's natural circadian rhythms can change again as they reach adulthood.[7]

Things to try…

- **Have a collaborative, problem-solving discussion with your child.** Validate and discuss all their ideas, even if they seem unrealistic, like "I'll just skip my first class." Talk with your child about both your concerns and theirs. Consider writing out the concerns as a list; this helps you keep track of them all and shows your child that you're hearing them and taking them seriously. Then, check each of the ideas you came up with together to see if they address everyone's concerns.[8]
- **Adjust the sensory environment in some way.** There are many ways to do this: use an alarm clock instead of waking your child up yourself (or vice versa); change the sound on the alarm clock to be harsher or softer; involve light by opening curtains, turning on a light, or using a sunrise alarm clock; involve taste or scent by cooking a breakfast that smells good (e.g., coffee or bacon), or perhaps by bringing the child a snack to eat or some juice to drink in bed before getting up… the list could go on and on.
- **Break down the steps of the morning routine into smaller segments, or rearrange their order.** For example, for one child, the thought of having to dress and brush their teeth before having any food may be overwhelming, and staying in bed instead is just too tempting. Rearranging the morning so breakfast comes first may make it easier for them to get up.

She's started letting out a huge, frustrated sigh whenever we ask her to do anything. The disrespect is really jarring, because she's always been so sweet and agreeable until now.

Listen, I'll do what you're asking me to, but you don't get to control how I feel about it, too. I've been following your directions for years and it's starting to grate on me, especially now that I have interests that are all my own, and I often feel like you don't understand me.

one possible child's point of view

Things to know…

- **A teenager's primary developmental job is to begin to differentiate themself from their parents.**[9] It's normal for them to start feeling more distant, like they need to push away from you. Along with that sometimes comes the feeling that parents are embarrassing or annoying—after all, it's much easier to push away someone who annoys or embarrasses you. These feelings are part of a growing, maturing brain, and are not a sign that anything is wrong with the relationship.
- People share their emotions for lots of reasons. **Not all of those reasons are intentional disrespect.** It may be tempting to take it personally when your child shares how they're feeling with you, but a lot of the time they're only thinking about how they're feeling—not about you at all. If they're feeling frustrated, they share their frustration; if they're feeling gloomy, they share their gloom. It's a natural instinct of social creatures.
- Often, but not always, **adults' feelings about being disrespected are rooted in their own childhood experiences.** If you had sighed or rolled your eyes at your parents, would you have been physically and emotionally safe? If not, it's likely that you feel unsafe when someone does the same thing to you.

Things to try…

- **Let your child start a dialogue with you about what is frustrating them,** if this is their attempt to initiate a conversation. If you decide to engage, get your own mindset into a helpful place first: the two of you are a team; it's not you versus your child. Try saying something like, "You seem to get really frustrated when I ask you to do this… what's up?"
- Maybe your child doesn't want to start a dialogue, and just wants to blow off steam. If so, sighing is a pretty safe way to express emotions without hurting anybody. **Remind yourself that it's not an emergency for your child to express themself in a childish way,** and doesn't actually require any response from you at all.
- If this type of situation happens consistently with the same factors, **find a different way to do whatever is frustrating you both.** For example, if you constantly seem to annoy your child by reminding them of a chore while they engage in a hobby, you could consider making a visual cue they can see, instead of issuing verbal reminders; reminding them at a different time of day; rearranging the chore distribution in the family; or any one of a dozen other potential solutions. (Enlisting your child as a problem-solving partner will probably be the most successful way to go about it![10])

He's started stealing. It feels big, scary, and serious. He took money out of my wallet and stole a trinket from his brother's room. I'm afraid for where this path leads.

I need this more than they do. I know it's wrong to take it but I don't know how else to get it. I need it, and I think no one will notice it's missing... but if someone does, we're family, so they'll have to forgive me, right?

Things to know…

- **Stealing things often comes from a feeling of needing to fight against helplessness.** There are many ways in which children don't have the power to get things they want. Adults can spend their money how they like, even foolishly or frivolously, but children are much more reliant upon their adults for the resources they are given, and even then, there are often restrictions on what they're allowed to use those resources for.
- **Stealing could also be a sign of lots of other things.** A child being bullied or peer-pressured may steal to try to impress or appease someone they think is their friend. A child with lagging impulse control could steal on a whim, without anything deep or sinister being behind it. A child who damaged a friend's property may steal a similar item to replace it, in a misguided attempt at taking responsibility. **Don't assume you know the whole story before you talk with your child.**

Things to try…

- **Have an honest discussion with your child about what's going on with them.** Don't come into the discussion already on the offensive; that will immediately put them on the defensive. As hard as it may be, try to remember that you are much more likely to succeed if you collaborate together to meet your child's need than if you react like they are a criminal or an enemy.
- **Truly listen to what they share with you, and don't rush to invalidate it,** even if it sounds factually untrue. If your child says something like, "I never have any money of my own to spend," don't immediately reply, "But what about the $20 you got from Grandma just last month?" Replying with corrections like this tells your child that your biggest concern is proving them wrong, not listening to how they feel. If you can't think of anything helpful to say, you could even reflectively repeat back, "It feels like you never have any money of your own to spend."
- Make it a priority, and make sure your child sees you making it a priority, to **find ways to work together with your child to legitimately obtain what they want.** Do this even if you feel that what they want is a waste of money or a silly thing to care about—for example, a power-up in a video game that costs real-world money. Assuming there are no legal issues with them having it, let them know that you two can work together to figure out how they can access it. If they're feeling restricted, misunderstood, and alone, they will only have themself to rely on in order to gain access to what they feel they need. But if they feel that you are on their side and will help empower them to earn what they need, they can channel that energy productively instead.

My child won't use manners at all. They just make demands of me and expect me to meet them. I'm so sick of being ordered around.

We have to use good manners for polite society—but we're not polite society here, right? I know everything about you, and you used to wipe my butt. Aren't we close enough that I can just tell you what I need?

Things to know…

- **People of all ages speak more comfortably at home than they do out in public.** If you were to watch a recording of yourself, you might be surprised by how rarely you say "please" or "thank you" to your family members versus when you're talking to someone at work, school, or the supermarket.
- When someone is unaware of something, **their brain may literally be not perceiving that thing.** This is true in all areas of life. If someone is unaware that wrinkly clothes look rumpled or unprepared, their brain may literally not process the visual information that typically leads a person to recognize wrinkles in a shirt. If someone is unaware of how voices with a particular sharpness to them are taken to indicate irritation, their brain may literally not hear the "rudeness" in their voice, or may hear it but not know how to modulate their vocal cords in order to filter it out.
- In a moment when your child needs something from you, **corrections are likely to feel like nitpicking.** They're focused on getting their need met, not learning about social nuances.

Things to try…

- At a separate time, **when you and your child are already feeling connected**—maybe when you're hanging out before bedtime or riding in the car—try casually bringing this up. "Hey, I'm not sure if you know this already, but the way you asked me to wash your soccer uniform earlier sounded like either something was wrong, or you were irritated with me. I wanted to check in and see if something was up." **They may not be attuned to the particulars of tone the way you are.**
- **Meet demands with authentic humor to defuse the tension.** "Oh yes, Your Majesty, I shall fetch you only the finest of water bottles, right away!" (Don't use this strategy if it can only come out of your mouth in a bitter or mocking way, or if your child wouldn't respond positively to this type of humor.)
- **Explain to your tween or teen what kinds of hormonal changes their brains and bodies are going through,** and how it's their job to start figuring out their identity during these years. **Let them know that you understand why they sometimes find you annoying or feel irritated,** even when there's no good reason to. You can even tell them stories about your own teenage years and the way you felt toward your parents, if appropriate to share.

I try being honest with him about how I've had a hard day at work and I just need to lie down on the couch for a little bit before I make dinner. I tell him he can make his own food if he doesn't want to wait. In response, he says I'm lazy and I do nothing all day. That hurts.

I'm exhausted, hungry, and prickly, and you expect me to praise you for giving the best of yourself to everybody ELSE all day long?!

I'm your kid. Take care of ME! Give your best to ME!

Things to know...

- **It's not a child's job to meet their parent's needs.** Yes, children can learn to be courteous, friendly, and even supportive—but ultimately, they cannot be who their parents depend on for emotional support.
- **Nobody is at their best when they're hungry or tired.** Try to avoid making long-term judgments about your kid as a person when either or both of you are tired and hungry!
- **Some kids don't like to be reminded that their parent devotes lots of attention and care to their job—i.e., not to the child.** The parent may believe that they're communicating, "I've had such a tough day at work, and need you to cooperate with me now," but their child hears, "I used up all my grace on other people and tasks (and not on you), so now I'm going to put more expectations on you."

Things to try...

- **Sometimes bad days call for emergency measures!** Order a pizza, put on a movie, play extra video games, stop by the gas station for snacks... do whatever it takes to give yourself *and* your kid one more hour of energy, instead of only one of you getting it at the other's expense. You can also acknowledge the bad day out loud. "It seems like we both had crummy days. Is there anything that we could do to fix that?" Approach the situation like, "We're in this together."
- When kids are little, **getting them in water or going outside** can often change the trajectory of a bad day. Sometimes these strategies can work for big kids or adults, too. Can one of you take a bubble bath? Can you go for a walk, whether alone or together?
- If you need to be off your feet for a minute, **use it as a connection opportunity:** invite your child to show you a video they like, show you some funny memes they've seen lately, or talk to you about something they are currently interested in.
- **Think about the five senses as a quick shorthand to give you ideas for small, "feel-good" sensory supports to turn the day around.** Can the two of you listen to something pleasant together, like music that you both like? How about lighting a candle or putting on a familiar, favorite show in the background?

She refuses to go to school. If I manage to drag her there, she refuses to do her homework—in fact, she won't even tell me that she HAS homework. She says she's got a stomachache every single day.

I really do mean it when I say I'm not feeling good, even though it happens a lot. People think I'm making it up or just being dramatic, but my body truly feels sick when I think about going places that overwhelm me. Please don't make me go… I don't know how to cope with these feelings.

one possible child's point of view

Things to know…

- **In many cases, anxiety requires professional intervention.** It is not just a feeling to "power through," and of course your child can't manage it alone. You can't fix it by yourself, either. Anxiety is a serious difficulty that often needs serious support. No matter what other people say, you know this to be true: neither you nor your child is making up how hard it is.
- Some schools are helpful, supportive, and kind. Other schools are unhelpful, unsupportive, and even hurtful. **Don't let a school district bully you** into forgetting that you and your child are on the same team.
- **You have rights as a parent.** The specific rights vary by country, state, province, or district, but most school districts are supposed to provide support, not punishment (at least on paper). It may be worth reaching out for help of some kind. Maybe you can find a local nonprofit chapter offering advocacy, a lawyer, a parent support group, an online discussion board, or something else. If you ask your school, they should also provide you with a printout explaining your legal rights and protections.

Things to try…

- **Listen to your child.** Don't brush them off or negate what they're saying (such as by listing all the things they love about school). Even if you feel nothing can be done, listen to them and hear what they're saying.
- **Guide your child in breaking down their concerns.** Is there a class or subject that is bothering them the most? Is the problem with a teacher, a student, or a particular expectation in that class? It's easier to solve a problem when you know, specifically, what the problem is.
- For some kids, it may help to **explain your local laws about school attendance,** or any other important factors that affect your family. This isn't to burden or scare your child with adult details that they have no control over, but rather to explain the reasoning behind societal rules about public education. Sometimes it can help to explain why the parent seems to be "siding with" the school.
- At a time when your child isn't already in crisis, **talk with them about how their anxiety feels in their body.** Maybe together you can come up with a sensory or emotional strategy that would help them manage the physical discomfort of living with anxiety, such as taking breaths along with a visual aid on an app; getting a tight, squeezy hug; or drinking something fizzy. At school, they might be able to try drinking ice-cold water, carrying a worry stone in their pocket, journaling about their emotions, or wearing a piece of fidget jewelry to channel nervous energy into movement.

My teenager never wants to spend time with us anymore. It's all about their friends or their sweetheart. If they do grace us with their presence, they're on their phone with their friends the whole time.

You're my nest, my safety. I'm growing up and naturally moving away from you. I'm safe and secure in my ability to return to you, which is why I'm clinging to my other relationships right now. Those relationships feel like they could vanish if I don't put all my time into maintaining them, but I know that you won't.

Things to know…

- **New relationships are full of feel-good hormones.** They're exciting in ways that existing, steady relationships aren't. Making a new friend is exciting, starting a new romantic relationship is exciting, and it's all even more so when there's an added element of growing up and doing new, mature things for the first time.
- It's a sign that your family culture has been successfully supportive if your growing teenager feels absolutely confident that their relationship with you is unshakeable. It might feel like a backhanded compliment if that comes in the form of blowing you off to hang out with other kids their age… but it really means **they know for sure you'll be there at the end of the day.** Their new relationships feel less stable, less secure. If the child doesn't devote their attention and self to the new relationship, it might fade away. But their parents? They're always going to be there.
- Throughout their teenage years, a child's entire job—their core identity development—is rooted in distancing themselves from their parents.[11] Which parts of themselves represent who they truly are, versus who their parents told them or raised them to be? No matter what their relationship with you has been like until now, teens (and even tweens) devote a lot of energy to figuring this out—**including spending lots of time with other sources of influence and information.**

Things to try…

- Think about what kind of interactions you're having with your child on any given day. Are they mostly positive, accepting, friendly, funny? Do you seek them out to share silly memes or videos, or something delightful that made you think of them during the day? **Try to emphasize those small moments of connection**—especially in comparison to how many times a day you ask them to do something, correct a behavior, or remind them of a responsibility.
- When your child does spend time with you, don't use it as an opportunity to make fun of them, complain about their new relationship, or lament how little time they spend with you these days. **Even good-natured teasing can really backfire and make a child feel like it would be easier to just avoid the conversation altogether.**

She expects perfection out of herself, much more than we expect from her. We try telling her that failure is a normal part of life, perfection doesn't exist, and she's perfect the way she is, but the words roll right off her.

Every time I try to talk about how I'm feeling, people rush to tell me I'm wrong. How can I explain myself without being told I'm "perfect the way I am"? Those words sound so fake. And how can I be perfect if "perfection doesn't exist," anyway?!

one possible child's point of view

Things to know...

- **Children often double down on expressing themselves if they feel unheard.** When our child comes to us with their uncomfortable feelings about themselves, it seems heartbreakingly obvious that we should simply reassure them about how perfect and wonderful they are to us! Unfortunately, our child may then walk away from the interaction feeling like we didn't even hear what they were saying. If they try to tell us again, they'll express it in an even stronger way—or they'll just give up and stop bringing these thoughts to us at all.
- **It is genuinely frustrating to be able to imagine amazing, perfect things and not have the skills to create them.** Yes, it takes time and hard work to polish a creative talent to a level of mastery. However, your child already has amazing ideas they wish they could execute *right now*, not after ten more years of practice. That's a really discouraging feeling!

Things to try...

- Empathetically reflect your child's feelings back to them. When they're ready, after you have heard about their feelings, **guide them through turning those feelings into action.** You could ask, "What do you wish was different about it?" or "What would you do differently next time?" and then help them create a plan based on those thoughts.
- **Chat with your child about the phrase "Try your best."** It's likely that many adults have said this to them throughout their lives—teachers, coaches, youth leaders, and so on. You may have said it yourself. Some children take this very literally, and believe they must perform at 100% of their capacity in everything they do. **This is a quick path to burning out!** Talk with your tween or teen about how people manage their energy.
  - **Acknowledge their efforts when you can:** "I'm sure you're exhausted from football earlier. No wonder it feels so hard to focus on your homework."
  - **Teach them to listen to their body's needs,** rather than pushing past their own breaking point. "You seem like you need a break from this work. What if we go for a short walk or have a snack and then come back to it?"
  - **Explain what success could look like in different scenarios**—and that it doesn't always look like perfection. "I'm actually thrilled that you got a B on this test! You know 85% of everything there is to know about World War II?! That's certainly more than I know about it!"

We have to get out the door at a set time for *her* activity. When that time comes, I'm sitting in the car waiting while she's still inside casually putting on makeup. It feels so disrespectful, and showing up late makes me anxious.

It's hard for me to remember all the steps it takes to do something. Like "getting ready to go" is actually so many smaller tasks, and it's hard to guess how long they'll all take me.

Things to know…

- **Time management is a big, tricky skill made up of lots of little skills.** Your child needs to understand when to leave the house, keep in mind all the small things they'll need to do before they leave, accurately estimate how long it takes to do all of those small things, and subtract that from the time they're planning to leave—all while not getting distracted and having to recalculate on the fly if they missed anything. That's a huge amount of mental energy devoted to managing a lot of moving pieces. (There's more detail on these little skills, which are collectively called *executive functioning*, in the appendix.)

Things to try…

- **Use online tools, such as GoblinTools, to break down a larger task into several smaller tasks.**[12] Showing your child how to use a tool like this also gives them the opportunity to manage it independently, which can feel less embarrassing or childish than your parent breaking down all the steps to getting out the door for you.
- **Give your child a stopwatch and have them measure how long it takes to do each of their "getting ready to go" tasks.** (Don't try this when you're already rushing to get out the door!) This helps your child create a more accurate mental estimate—maybe brushing their hair actually takes twice as long as your child predicted, or picking out clothes takes extra time because your tween or teen wants to reevaluate what they'd like to wear.
- Don't treat your child's independent choices as if they are the problem. It could be tempting to tell your child, "You don't need to spend an hour putting on makeup," but this only reinforces that you don't understand what's important to them. Instead, **focus your problem-solving efforts on figuring out how to make time for your child to meet their needs.** "What if you put on makeup first, and we take your breakfast with us in the car and you eat it on the way?"

We're not bothered by curse words in our house, but lately my child wants to use them nonstop for pointless things. Nobody is modeling that for them, so I don't know why they're so fixated on these words.

If taking it this far is funny, how about *this* far?!

I love it when my parents play along (seeing old people curse is hilarious!), but it's just as funny when they don't and get super mad—all because of the words *I'm* saying!

one possible child's point of view

Things to know…

- **Humor develops from boundary-pushing and doing the unexpected.** When children grow into tweens and teenagers, a massive amount of their play becomes verbal and social rather than being as physical as it used to be when they were younger.[13] Part of this playfulness is experimenting with humor, and a big part of humor is experimenting with what's offensive versus delightfully surprising.
- **Teenagers play with language the way toddlers play with objects.** It's like the scientific method: "If I drop this [object/f-bomb], what happens? What if I do it over here? What about outside? What about at home, at school, on the bus, or in public…?"
- Even when they're teenagers, huge portions of children's lives are dictated to them by adults. They live in and move through different social spheres for home, school, and community, and each sphere has its own system that selectively doles out control and autonomy. But **language is something other humans cannot control.** Adults can police or punish language choices, but they cannot stop anyone from saying anything. For this reason, teenagers who feel overcontrolled in other areas may choose to experiment with their power in what they say.

Things to try…

- Determine for yourself what your family boundaries are. **Involve your child in the discussion to create them if you can,** or clearly communicate these boundaries to your child if you can't. Some families expect that no one will say curse words; other families may allow them at specific times, or in some settings but not others; still other families may allow only some kinds of cursing, such as cursing in pain or surprise, but not at another person. Make sure you understand your own reasoning, and then share your reasoning with your child.
- **Hold yourself to the same standards as your child.** If it's important that nobody in your family curses, include yourself in that. It's unreasonable to expect your child to uphold ideals you aren't modeling yourself.
- **Consider letting it go entirely.** Your child may simply hold different values than you do, and the teenage years are a key time for exploring and expressing your values. You can provide your child with factual information— "You might get in trouble at school if you say that around Mr. Smith"—and let them navigate the rest however they choose.

We have a big family, and our oldest is better at playing with the babies than the middles. The oldest will sometimes fight with our middle children, which is absurd! They don't need to be fighting kids who are years younger than they are.

Babies are easy for me to understand and get along with. It's way harder to relate to someone who was once my playmate, but is nothing like my friends now. Some days it feels so frustrating to even live in the same house as someone so childish.

one possible child's point of view

Things to know…

- **During the teenage years, friends eclipse families as the most important influence in a child's life.** It's natural for teenagers to distance themselves from their families as they try to establish their identity in other roles that have nothing to do with their family role.
- Babies are more predictable than older children. Babies typically have a few simple needs and desires, while older children want more complicated forms of socialization, play, and interaction. **A lot of people prefer babies to toddlers or older children, which is okay.**

Things to try…

- Remember that siblings' relationships are not something you can directly control—just like the relationships between any other two people. **What you can do is set them up for success as much as possible.** Invite the whole family to do an activity that both children like. Activities that incorporate whole-body movement (such as going for a nature walk, playing Frisbee, biking, skateboarding, playing mini golf, and so on) may work well for a family of varying ages and abilities. Water-based activities (like swimming, wading in a creek, or playing with a sprinkler) are another good "middle ground" option for different ages of children and adults.
- **When problem-solving, try to pinpoint particular issues.** "My oldest and my middle child never get along" is so broad as to be nearly impossible to begin unpuzzling. "My oldest gets frustrated when we are all riding in the car together to get groceries on the weekends and my middle child talks endlessly about his hobbies" is far more concrete. The more specific you can get with a problem, the more solutions you can come up with.[14]
- **Make sure to avoid putting all the responsibility on the eldest child.** It's really hard to watch one of our children do something that seems mean or hurtful to another of our children, because to a parent, it feels like watching one child be attacked—we want to leap to their defense. As long as your child isn't actually being attacked, try to stick to moderating or coaching your kids through fights, especially if you're tempted to always take the side of the youngest. **The oldest is still your baby too.**

He constantly throws out self-deprecating or negative comments while trying to do his schoolwork. I try to stay positive and affirming, but it's hard to battle the stream of negativity.

The harder I try to tell my parent that I suck at this and I feel stupid, the harder they double down on telling me I'm smart and I can do it. I'm overwhelmed by this work, and I'm conveying that the best way I know how! I'm not fishing for platitudes or pep talks; I just want someone to see how difficult this is for me.

Things to know...

- **People often use the strongest language they know to express the strongest emotions they feel.** Your child may be trying very hard to express their feelings to you, which is a good thing—we want our tweens and teens to feel like they can come to us to talk about how they're feeling!

Things to try...

- **Don't negate what your child is saying.** If your child says, "I can't get this, I'm so stupid," and you say, "You're not stupid, you can do it," you've just contradicted everything your child is trying to share with you, effectively shutting down further conversation.
- **Reflect back what you hear:** "This is so hard, it's making you feel stupid." Listening to what your child is saying doesn't mean agreeing with them that they're bad at something—it just means recognizing discouragement as a normal human emotion, and empathetically agreeing with how hard it is to feel that way.
- Consider your current homework setup. **Would something else work better for your child or family at this time?** If homework is causing intense frustration or discouragement, or is getting in the way of other important things like sleep, family time, or time to rest and play, think hard about whether the expectations could change.
  - You could **have a meeting with your child's teacher(s)** or school administrators about their workload.
  - You could change your own expectations of your child to **allow them to skip homework,** or work on it for only a set amount of time before stopping.
  - Your child could **complete a portion of each assignment** to make sure they understand the concepts: for example, doing only three of the math problems rather than all fifteen.
  - You could **provide more support for your child,** such as by sitting alongside them as a support partner while they work, or finding a peer, tutor, or other person to fill that role for them. Even if this particular school subject isn't your strong suit, your child may find initiating a task and moving through all its steps much more doable with someone else by their side. This concept, called *body doubling*, is absolutely vital for some types of brains.
  - You could **be more hands-off with your child's schoolwork,** giving them the space to make their own decisions and independently manage their own work.

Key themes from these years:

1. Even though it may feel like your child is *just* about to enter adulthood, you still don't have to worry about who they might be tomorrow or as adults. **It's okay to focus on what the child in front of you today needs from you today.** They are not done growing and maturing yet. (Even adults continue to grow and mature!)

2. When something isn't working for you and your big kid, **the two of you are the best possible team to come up with a solution that will work for you specifically.** Collaborating to solve a problem is the best way to determine whether a plan will meet both your kid's needs and your needs. There are a wealth of resources about how to do this.[15]

3. **It's hard to be a big kid.** Tweens and teens sometimes live in a no-win scenario. When they are silly or playful, or they make a childish mistake, they're expected to have acted more mature and grown-up. But when they take something seriously, pursue a romantic relationship, or talk about what's important to them, they're brushed off because they're still a child. **Try to remember that push-pull feeling.** You may have felt that way yourself once upon a time, or you might just have to imagine it. Your teenager may seem young to you, but they are the oldest they've ever been, and the things that feel important feel the most important that anything's ever felt.

4. Emotions are tumultuous in the teenage years. For most children, teenage sadness feels like the biggest and deepest sadness they have ever felt. It's the same story for anger, irritation, fear, joy, etc. Learning that all emotions, even the uncomfortable ones, are survivable is an ongoing journey. It's still not your job as a parent to make sure your child only feels comfortable emotions; **it is your job to make sure that your child knows they can come to you in the middle of the storm.**

5. Tweens and teens still have some of the difficulties they had as younger children, too. They may use language in non-literal ways. They may not modulate their tone or nonverbal cues quite right to get their message across correctly. They may want independence in some tasks but not be good at doing those tasks independently yet. These statements all describe teenagers, toddlers, and any age group in between. That is because **tweens and teens are still children.** They are still learning.

Notes

[1]Nucci, "Development of Moral Reasoning."

[2]Einzig, "It's All My Fault."

[3]Wise, "Dopamine."

[4]Cools et al., "Dopamine."

[5]Wolfson and Carskadon, "Sleep Schedules."

[6]Wolfson and Carskadon.

[7]Wolfson and Carskadon.

[8]Greene, *Raising Human Beings.*

[9]Erikson, *Childhood and Society.*

[10]Greene, *Raising Human Beings.*

[11]Erikson, *Childhood and Society.*

[12]GoblinTools, "Magic ToDo."

[13]Hughes, *A Playworker's Taxonomy.*

[14]Greene, *Raising Human Beings.*

[15]Greene.

At School

(All Ages)

the adult's point of view

My student won't let anybody else share the spotlight. Whenever someone else gets to lead the line, gets called on to answer a question, or gets praised by an adult, this student cries or tries to insert themself into the situation. They don't get what they want by acting this way, but even when we ignore the behavior, they don't stop.

I love it when school makes me feel special. When school makes me feel left out instead, it makes me so sad that I cry. The adults scoff and think I'm crying to "get something," but I'm crying because it hurts to feel left out.

one possible student's point of view

102

Things to know...

- **Human beings need connection and closeness with other human beings.** Closeness is a very literal hallmark of safety for us—we feel physically and emotionally unsafe when we feel disconnected from others. A student who is desperately seeking attention is really seeking (emotional) safety. For many students, the most reliable place to feel that sense of connection and belonging is at school.
- **Ignoring someone who is seeking attention only reinforces the feelings of being unsafe** that are leading them to cling so hard to connection with others in the first place.
- When children are overwhelming with their connection needs, **it's often because they struggle to continue to feel a connection when it isn't actively being affirmed.** To put it another way, they feel loved as long as someone is saying "I love you," but the moment the person stops saying it, they fear the love has stopped too.

Things to try...

- **Make time to connect meaningfully and one-on-one with your student.** The best times to do this are often outside of teaching times: stand next to your student in the hallway while they hang up their backpack, spend a moment beside their table at breakfast or lunch, or chat with them as they come in from the bus. A popular strategy, "Two by Ten," involves speaking to one particular student for two minutes each day, for ten consecutive days, about anything in their life other than school and academics.[1] With the teacher conveying, "You are personally important to me, and I will make space to hear about your life and thoughts," the student may feel less of a need to grasp for that attention and connection in other parts of the day.
- **Develop a ritual with the student that conveys connection in a small, quick, non-disruptive way:** for example, a hand signal, a facial expression, or a visual to show. It could be something very specific, like putting a card with positive phrases on their desk that you can tap wordlessly as you walk by; it could also be as simple as giving a thumbs-up, wink, or nod to the student to acknowledge, **"I see you, I know this is hard for you, and I want you to remember we're still on the same team."**
- **Affirm to your students that feeling sad is okay.** Sadness is much more overwhelming to children when it also feels shameful and like it needs to be hidden. Believing that "all feelings are allowed" necessarily involves accepting that some classroom decisions make some children feel sad.

I have a student who makes constant noise in class. We talk about indoor voices, working silently, and how they're disturbing the other students. Nothing works! They can't stay quiet for even thirty seconds.

When I make sounds, it feels better inside my body. I'm not even really aware of when I'm doing it. It just feels "right," the same way that continuing to breathe feels better than holding my breath.

one possible student's point of view

Things to know…

- **Children making noise often has more to do with their sensory processing skills than their behavior.** (This is actually true for a lot of "behaviors" for which the child is able to verbally tell you a rule, but then seems to ignore it.) Their body is meeting a sensory need, and that instinct is overriding their logical or verbal reasoning abilities. It doesn't mean they are remembering the rule and yet intentionally choosing to ignore it—rather, it means that their brain isn't thinking of the rule at all as it seeks out what it needs to feel safe or feel good. (The appendix at the end of the book has lots more information about sensory processing.)
- Some people make noise because they are seeking sensory input. **They want to hear more sound with their ears, or they want more touch, pressure, or movement from their mouth or hands** (depending on what they're using to make sound).
- Some people make noise because they are avoiding sensory input. **The sound they are making is to cover up, or distract themselves from, a sound that is bothering them.**

Things to try…

- **Do some detective work around why the student is making noise.** This will help you figure out what substitution could work for this child. Someone who hums to themself to drown out the sound of a distantly rattling air conditioner may respond well to white noise or soft music in the classroom that also masks the annoying sound. Someone who drums on the table and beatboxes while they work may need a lot more movement to be able to focus—maybe they could stand on a wobble board beside their desk while they write.
- Don't assume the child is aware that they're making noise. Often, humans meet their own sensory needs subconsciously. **You may have to provide consistent, gentle reminders, in addition to a replacement way to meet their need, before the child is able to stop.** That doesn't mean they're ignoring you or being bad. They need to receive the message that it's normal and natural to meet their body's needs, and that you're there to help them do so in a way that meets *everybody's* needs.

My students ask me all the time, "Why do we have to learn this? We can just look up anything we want to know." They act like they were born already knowing everything there is to know, and they don't need school. I try to be gracious with any corrections, and I'm met with opposition anyway. I'm tired of having to justify everything I'm teaching them!

The adults never give reasons that make sense for why we have to learn all this. How do we know they're being realistic about what our futures are going to look like? They're picturing "ye olden times" when they didn't always have easy access to the collective knowledge of all of humanity. They're out of touch with us. So, we'll keep asking: why *do* we need to know this?

Things to know...

- **This is a pretty good question.** When you were a student, did a math teacher ever tell you, "You're not going to have a calculator everywhere you go"? And yet here you are, most likely, with a smartphone in your pocket! It's forward-thinking for children to realize that the world of the future will look very different from the world of the present, and this consideration is a sign of a maturing brain.
- **Questioning authority figures is also a sign of maturity.** Sure, it's frustrating when you're the authority figure —but it's wise for human beings to ask why, when someone tells them to do something. Kids ask questions when they are thinking for themselves, which is a good thing!

Things to try...

- **Give your students chances to be experts.** Children are born learners; they probably know quite a lot about some topic they love, whether that's the Bermuda Triangle, dolphins, Pokémon, or the history of their favorite band. **Find ways to connect your teaching to the things they love.** Show them how literacy, science, history, and math permeate the things that delight them.
- **Work together to discover the "why" behind the things we have to do.** Avoid "slippery slope" arguments and consider what's actually meaningful to a child—"You have to learn math because everyone needs math in their life" may feel abstract, but "Knowing about probabilities helps you understand the mechanics behind random loot drops in your favorite video game" may be a reason the child can connect to.
- **Reframe the question in your mind.**
  - Does it help if you hear it as a form of curiosity instead of attitude? Imagine if your students knew how to say, in an earnest tone of voice, "I'd love to know how the skills and lessons you're teaching me could become the foundations of the things I dream of doing someday! Can you tell me more about that?" **Try answering your students as if they're truly curious.**
  - **Sometimes a question like this is a bid for adult perspective.** "I want to participate, but I can't get my brain to make the motivation for me to do it, because this feels arbitrary. Do you know anything about this topic that can help me get over that obstacle?"

the adult's point of view

Correcting him doesn't work; consequences don't work; losing recess doesn't work. He repeats the same behavior over and over as if he has no idea what he's doing wrong, when we *just* talked about it!

Adults must not like me, or must be out to get me. I don't understand why they keep targeting me, taking things away from me, and getting mad and yelling at me. They do it over and over for no reason. Maybe I'm a bad person.

one possible student's point of view

Things to know…

- You've already noticed that consequences don't work. **Escalating the consequences won't make them suddenly start working.**
- **Tools like punishment or behavioral strategies "work" by putting a child into a state of fear, and hoping the fear overrides their developmental capabilities or their needs.** Most schools don't actually want to do this to children. This strategy does not foster long-term growth, because eventually a situation will arise in which the fear won't outweigh the child's desire to get their needs met.
- Children are immature and cannot always accurately put themselves into an adult's mindset. For many children, their biggest takeaway from being punished is simply, "They must not like me." **This only harms the relationship between the adult and the child,** and creates even less of a reason for the child to cooperate—would you want to obey the commands of someone who you believed personally disliked you?

Things to try…

- **Assume that children want to do well,** and that if they are struggling, it's because something is in their way. Dr. Ross Greene's body of work expounds on this concept, and he has created an entire framework for collaborative problem solving with a child; his book *Lost at School* would be a great place for an educator to start.[2]
- **Consider the student's executive functioning skills.** Are they able to pay attention to what you're saying for long enough to comprehend the rules? Can they remember all the steps of a complex set of directions, or does their working memory forget anything that came after step one? Do they know how to ask for help when they're confused, or do they believe they should just guess what comes next? **Children may appear to be "misbehaving" when really there is a gap in comprehension.**
- **Never take away recess!** Elementary-aged children need three hours of unstructured outdoor play per day.[3] Most children get *far* less than that. Taking away the slim amount they do get as a punishment only makes the problem worse, because now the child is missing out on body movement, energy exertion, time for their brains to relax and think their own thoughts, and so much more.

My student is aggressive at school. Even when he's not hitting or throwing things, he still puts his hands on the other kids too often. He has no boundaries and we hate it.

"Kind hands"… "We don't hit our friends"… I've heard it all before, but I can't *remember* that stuff when I'm mad! Can't you see I'm really struggling with the other kids here? Is anybody going to ask me what's making it so hard for *me* to be around all these other kids?!

one possible student's point of view

Things to know...

- **Focusing on the "misbehavior" is missing the point.** In the moment that your student is in crisis, yes, you need to stop them from hurting other students. But when the student isn't actively in crisis, focusing on the behaviors that occur during the crisis is looking too far down the road. Schools must work to support students *before* they reach a crisis point by focusing on the patterns, triggers, and interactions that lead up to that point.
- **Some students have strong sensory systems that interpret even light touch as a threat.** These students often appear to be "aggressive" because the adults see children hitting, shoving, or yelling out of nowhere. But from the child's perspective, the person who brushed against them while walking by is the one who instigated it, and **they were reacting to defend themself.**
- Rough-and-tumble play is a developmental need during the preschool and elementary school years.[4] It is also a developmentally normal way that children learn self-regulation skills. Schools may have to limit this type of play for safety reasons, but **we can't fault children for seeking to meet normal needs and learn normal skills.**

Things to try...

- **Make sure the student can trust that they'll receive help if they ask for it.** Schools often teach students, "Use your words to ask for help." However, when a child does ask for help, they may be questioned about the legitimacy of their request, blamed for instigating the problem, told to try to solve it themselves first, or ignored (even temporarily) while the adult deals with something else. **Prioritize responding to a struggling student's verbal bids for help,** even when they ask imperfectly, while they're learning that self-advocacy is useful and that the adults can be on their team.
- Sometimes a visual activity can help kids conceptualize personal boundaries. **Give everybody a hula hoop to demonstrate how far apart people typically like to stand from other people,** unless they've agreed to be closer or play together.
- **Offer students more whole-body movement and play throughout the day to help meet some of the sensory needs** that aggressive behavior can stem from. Try taking the class outside to write in their literacy workbooks, having them hunt around the room for math fact cards, or joining them in doing jumping jacks to wake up brains and wiggle bodies.

the adult's point of view

When we say it's time to line up, she insists on being next to the "right" peer in line, or else she'll go sit back down at her seat and say she isn't going. She does it when we're going somewhere she doesn't like, too.

There's an awful lot I can't control during the school day, but I've figured out one thing: they can't *force* me to move my body in ways I don't like, or to go places I don't want to go.

one possible student's point of view

Things to know...

- Most school districts do not let adults physically move children who are not in danger, so **the child is correct that this is an area where they have power!** The adults need to approach the student with a teamwork mentality, not a control mentality—especially when they literally cannot use force.
- Kids' brains are working hard all the time to predict what will happen next. **Some children have a harder time recovering from moments when their predictions were revealed to be wrong.** It feels like all that work they just did was for nothing, and now their brain has to start over again and create a new plan.

Things to try...

- **Try assigning the child a special job in line:** hold the door, lead the line, carry the clipboard, etc. If the job can stay the same for a while, that may also help by creating predictability around how the transition will look.
- **Create a buddy system for when it's time to line up.** Each student has one peer who they're partnered with for the week. When it's time to go, they line up with their buddy! **Sometimes, challenging moments in life are easier to get through with a friend by our side.**
- **Come up with playful "assignments" for going places in line.** For example, everybody looks for something red while walking in the hallway, or everybody counts how many doorknobs they walk past. This provides a distraction technique and helps you **clearly communicate something the students *can* do, rather than only what they *can't* do.**
- **Avoid making empty threats.** If a student says, "I'm not going," and the adult replies, "Fine, then we're going without you," when the adult is literally *not allowed* to do that, they're usually betting on frightening the child into complying quickly to avoid being left behind. If the child doesn't give in, now the adult has put themself into an even more powerless position.
- **Imagine that the child is having a physical crisis of some kind.** If the student was unable to walk with the class because they were bleeding or having a seizure, no one would threaten them or get into a power struggle with them—adults would approach compassionately to figure out what was wrong and try to help. **Approach a child in emotional crisis the same way.**

I work with students in the special education program, and they say that I must think they're stupid when I give them work that's at their level. They think of it as "baby work"—they know they're different—but if I give them harder work, they can't do it. I just want to do what's right for them.

I know everybody thinks I'm stupid, but at least I'm not so stupid that I don't even *know* I'm stupid. You can't make me do baby stuff. I have more dignity than that.

one possible student's point of view

Things to know…

- **Disabled humans of all ages are often infantilized by the able-bodied people they encounter throughout the day.** The students' feelings of annoyance are probably rooted in very real lived experiences.
- The "just right challenge" is an occupational therapy concept that describes the way clients progress through therapy when they face challenges that feel tough enough to be motivating, but still achievable.[5] This concept works in the school setting as well. Students may express this type of frustration when they're not given the "just right challenge." **The work feels so easy, it's demotivating.**

Things to try…

- **Tailor students' work to their interests.** Include details from their favorite video game in mathematical word problems. Ask them to analyze the grammar in their favorite singer's lyrics. Have them practice writing down what they would say if they were creating their own YouTube channel. There are a million ways to open doors for students and show them that school skills are woven into the things they already love.
- **Talk about different kinds of intelligence:** for example, how some people excel at moving their bodies precisely how they want to, some people master language and expressing themselves, some people create incredible art, and so on.[6]
- Whenever possible, invite your students to evaluate their own work, their own thoughts, and their own creations, rather than relying on the judgment of other people. When they finish something, ask them with delight to tell you about it, rather than jumping to praise it. **Praise can be uplifting, but it also reinforces that your students need you to tell them how they've done.** When you make space for them to self-reflect first, they learn to hear their own pride in themselves before they hear *your* voice.
- Take that too-easy assignment and add an element to make it slightly more involved, difficult, or engaging. **For example, you could try adding multiple steps, a timer, or movement.** One child may be offended by adding basic numbers, but may enjoy timing themselves to see how quickly they can complete ten addition problems. Another child may bristle at practicing spelling basic words, but may be excited to "practice typing" with the same spelling list.

She runs out of the room for no reason at all. We set up a calm-down corner for her to take a break if she needs it, but she'd rather go running down the hallway, or even out of the school building. It's dangerous.

I have to get out of here. Nobody understands I'm in danger. I have to run away. My life depends on it!

Things to know…

- **People run away when they are afraid.** When trying to safeguard a student who frequently runs away, keep in mind that children don't do things "for no reason." Very often, a child runs away because they feel unsafe, anxious, or threatened by something in the environment, whether that's a person, a sensory trigger, an expectation, or something else.
- Some children do run (or "elope," in behaviorist terms) for other reasons as well. **You can take a child's emotions seriously and consider whether there could be other reasons,** such as:
  - The child does not understand what is expected of them and **follows their own impulse instead,** or their impulse to run is stronger than their desire to do what is expected of them.
  - The child has a lot of movement energy uncomfortably trapped in their body and **is trying to listen to their body's needs.**
  - **Something or someone the child wants very badly** is in a different place.
  - The child is **seeking connection with their adults** by trying to engage them in play.

Things to try…

- Reconsider using the classroom's "calm-down corner" for this student. A child who is running away, whether in fear or for fun, is meeting some kind of a need. **Redirecting them to a place where they must sit still might not meet that need.** Can you instead redirect them to another place where they can pace or jump? Can you designate a place in the school for them to run *toward,* such as a counselor's office, if they feel unsafe?
- **Examine the triggering events.** Look for an emotional or thematic pattern that emerges from the times when the child runs.
  - If a child runs away when they're asked to do something, **doing it likely feels physically or emotionally impossible for them.** Find a different way—maybe the child could choose one of three things to do, or do the task with a partner.
  - If a child runs away during transition times, like when the class moves from doing one thing to another, having a partner or special transition object (like a fidget tool or small stuffed animal to carry) may help **distract their brain from the impulse to run.**
  - If a child runs away "for no reason," **pay attention to the sensory environment.** Maybe a sound, sight, smell, or touch is overwhelming the child, and they are fleeing as if under attack. (A school occupational therapist can help with this analysis and make suggestions to adjust the environment.)

the adult's point of view

One kid is ruining twenty-nine other kids' day, every day. The school administration won't remove or discipline him, so we're all just forced to tolerate him.

I'm in so much distress, my body is wholly focused on protecting itself. I'm alone here, aren't I? Everybody else acts like it's all of them versus me, so it must be true. I will do whatever I have to do to feel safe, since I obviously have to fend for myself.

one possible student's point of view

Things to know...

- **School requires more out of some kids than others.** For some kids, going to school means going to a lovely, cheerful place filled with people who like them, and where they get to tackle exciting challenges. For other kids, going to the exact same school means dragging themselves somewhere too bright and too loud, to spend time around people who can barely stand to be in their presence, and where they're expected to fail at tasks repeatedly.
- **Making children feel worse will not make them behave better.** Stay away from interventions that seek to make a child feel so bad that they'll magically acquire skills they don't actually have. Punishment—like taking away recess or break times, or excluding the child from rewards for good behavior—is founded on this principle.
- The classroom culture has a huge impact on how the other twenty-nine kids process what's happening every day. **The adults set the tone for whether everyone fears and blames the "troublemaker,"** or whether everyone knows that we all need extra help sometimes.

Things to try...

- Somebody needs to bond with this child. It could be a teacher—maybe one who doesn't have to teach them all day long. It could be a counselor, principal, or receptionist. It could be a custodian or someone who works in the lunchroom. It may be easiest for the child to bond with somebody who has absolutely nothing to do with school discipline. But **this child absolutely needs somebody who simply lights up to see them,** who tells them they missed them when they were gone.
- **Develop a greeting or ritual with the student.** It could be a call-and-response, like "See you later, alligator/In a while, crocodile." It could be an inside joke or a silly nickname. Interpersonal rituals are like a secret shortcut to making people feel like they belong somewhere, and this child needs to feel like they belong.
- **Create a means of appropriate escape for the child and teach them how to use it.** The way this looks will vary depending on the setting and the child's age. **A child who feels trapped feels like they have to fight;** a child who knows they can escape can begin to access options besides fighting to keep themself safe.
  - **Escaping could mean leaving the room,** such as excusing themself to the restroom to take a break, or to the front office to go see the counselor.
  - **Escaping could mean leaving the area,** such as going to hide away in a calm-down corner.
  - **Escaping could mean emotionally, mentally, or sensorily "checking out,"** such as putting on noise-canceling headphones, reading a book, or doodling instead of doing the classroom activity.
  - **The child should never get in trouble for choosing to escape rather than to fight.**

No matter what the assignment is, she does the bare minimum. She's perfectly capable of doing more to challenge herself. When I ask her to do more, though, she responds in a disrespectful way.

I already ANSWERED the question. I already GAVE you what you wanted. Now you're coming back and telling me to do even more?! UGH!

one possible student's point of view

Things to know…

- **It's a very high-level skill to be able to picture a completed project in your mind, then start from the beginning and work all the way to the end.** Many children have a hard time picturing what a finished project will look like, and exactly how to get there. This student may be really discouraged that they successfully carried out the plan they had in their head, only to find out that their concept of "finished" didn't match what was expected of them all along. (This is an executive functioning skill, and there are more details about that skill set in the appendix.)

- Imagine if you were doing the dishes, and you finally completed the very last one, dried it, and put it away. Then a family member came into the room with twenty stinky, food-crusted plates and forks from another room that you hadn't even known about, and they expected you to wash those too before you were allowed to be done. **How might you feel?** A child who believes they've done everything that's expected of them, and then finds out that there are other expectations too, is probably experiencing the same feeling!

Things to try…

- **Clearly lay out the expectations for an assignment before it begins.** Ask yourself what your assignment is trying to measure. Consider that there are different ways to convey expectations: for example, a teacher who wants their students to practice writing three-sentence paragraphs might ask for three sentences, no matter how long they take, while a teacher who wants their students to practice writing for fifteen minutes might ask for fifteen minutes, no matter how many sentences they get. (A third teacher who wants their students to brainstorm all possible ideas about a topic might ask their students to write sentences, draw pictures, jot down notes, or dictate their thoughts to a voice recorder!)

- **Give an example of what "finished" looks like.** Whether that means showing a picture, demonstrating the steps of the assignment for your students, or having an example displayed somewhere in the classroom for reference, the concreteness of a visual model helps students understand expectations.

- Whenever possible, **don't get bogged down in the nuances of emotional expression.** Students who sigh and roll their eyes are still learning how to cope with disappointed or disgusted feelings while remaining cooperative. Changing the subject to nitpick about their tone and feelings when they're already frustrated is never helpful.

My student lies about everything all the time. This is costing them friendships, because people don't want to be around them after their lies are revealed. It's causing drama, and I can't figure out why they keep doing it.

I'm worried that the true stuff I have to share won't interest anybody, but when I tell my cool stories, everybody starts listening! The glow I feel while everyone is interested in me outweighs the crash that happens later when they get annoyed with me.

one possible student's point of view

Things to know…

- **There are lots of reasons students might lie.** Some of these reasons might be:
    - **The student enjoys seeming interesting to others** when they say outrageous things.
    - **The student is anxious about telling the truth,** fearing that doing so will get them in trouble, cause them to lose friends, or otherwise make them feel unsafe.
    - **The student is attempting to be humorous or exciting,** and does not have a good understanding of where the line between playful exaggeration and deceit is.
    - **The student is very impulsive** and is saying whatever comes into their head.
    - **The student is trying to convey the depth of their emotions.** For example, a student whose father is away on a business trip might tell people their father died, if people's reactions to the news of a death would feel more in line with how much the student misses their father than if they told the truth.

Things to try…

- **Make an effort to connect with the child,** such as by using the "Two by Ten" technique—speak to one challenging student for two minutes, for ten days in a row, about anything in their life other than school and academics.[7] As the teacher communicates, "I want to hear about your life and thoughts because you personally matter to me," the child may feel less of a need to grasp for the attention that outrageous storytelling brings.
- Depending on the child's age and level of understanding, you may be able to **defuse the situation with good humor.** "Oh wow, what a story! **You have such a great imagination.** If you were writing this as a book, what would you make happen next?"
- **Talk with everyone about how we can determine if something is true.** If someone makes an outlandish claim, what kinds of evidence might help back that claim up (or prove it wrong)? We live in an ever-changing world that includes technology that can create photos and even videos of things that didn't happen, making it more important than ever for children to learn how to critically evaluate information for truthfulness.
- **Have a private conversation with the child—not a confrontation or accusation.** You could try saying something like, "I heard you talking about this earlier. I thought, 'That sounds like a big story!' Do you want to tell me anything more about it?"

the adult's point of view

My student cannot transition from one activity to another. We give ten-minute, five-minute, and one-minute warnings, but they still freak out when it's time to be done. They won't help the class clean up from the activity so we can move on, either.

I'm much more interested in what I'm doing now than whatever comes next. I'm really focused on my work and not ready to break my focus yet. You may be able to force me to stop doing this thing I love, but you certainly can't force me to *help* you take it away!

one possible student's point of view

Things to know...

- Some children have shorter attention spans; some children can focus for quite a long time. **Either way, it can feel very uncomfortable to have your focus interrupted.**
- **Being at school is often an exercise in ignoring and filtering out irrelevant stimuli.** Students aren't expected to stop working every time a classmate coughs, someone sharpens a pencil, or another class walks by in the hallway, yet they're expected to stop working immediately when told to by a teacher. The process of learning which auditory input to filter out and which to attend to can take some time.
- **School is absolutely full of transitions, far more than most adults realize.** Adults can often pinpoint the big ones, like moving from the classroom to the lunch room, but may forget about the dozens or even hundreds of times each day that children are corrected; redirected; moved from one task to the next; rotated through stations, centers, and class subjects; and so on. For children whose brains tend to take longer to warm up to a new subject, especially those who become deeply rooted in their work once they do get started, it can be jarring, frustrating, or outright intolerable to be made to transition so often.

Things to try...

- Depending on the child's age and developmental ability, they may or may not have a concept of how long a minute is. **Transition warnings that are more concrete,** like "Everybody pick one more question to answer" or "We're going to play one song and then clean up," may be more appropriate.
- **Sometimes involving an object in the transition is helpful.** If a student is expected to play with toy dinosaurs, then put them all away, the transition is not only jarring but also sad: they have to say goodbye to something they love. If the student is instead allowed to put away all the dinosaurs but one, and that one can "walk" to lunch with them, the transition may be easier for them to manage.

Key themes from this setting:

1. **Teaching has a lot of unique challenges, but the core themes of respect, collaboration, and reciprocity are just as important as they are in parenting.** Teachers can't always interact with children the way they might if they were parenting—they can't pick up a child and move them, and they have to juggle thirty sets of needs instead of just a few. But kids at school want to be safe and loved just as badly as kids at home do, and building a relationship by connecting with the kids is still the best way to show them that they're safe and loved.

2. There is a pervasive feeling of rushing and urgency at school that really works against both teachers and kids. School standards and strict administrative expectations often leave teachers feeling like they have absolutely no leeway. When it's time to move from one thing to the next, everybody must move immediately; when it's time to stop working, everybody must stop working immediately; and when it's time to stop crying, everybody must stop crying immediately. **Unfortunately, urgency is the opposite of childhood.** Anytime adults can protect kids' right to do things at their own pace, children thrive.

3. Some children have a very, very hard time at school. These children often follow a trajectory that sounds like: **"Nobody understands me… nobody likes me… and it's all my fault."** It takes time for this entire belief to grow, and there are opportunities to intervene as the belief is still developing but not solidified yet. We can find ways to make sure we understand the child. We can find ways to convey that we like the child, even when they are challenging. **We must meaningfully connect with them before the whole sentence is complete and then codified into their self-talk.**

4. Much like in parenting, it's tempting to project into the future and imagine that a child who is struggling with something right now will suffer someday if they're not corrected. Also much like in parenting, **it's very freeing to let go of that fear and instead focus on meeting the child's needs exactly as they are right now.** Their future selves will still be ready to face challenges, develop skills, and find ways to meet their own needs.

Notes

1Wlodkowski, *Motivation and Teaching.*
2Greene, *Lost at School.*
3Hanscom, *Balanced and Barefoot.*
4Hughes, *A Playworker's Taxonomy.*
5Molineux, *Dictionary of Occupational Science.*
6Checkley, "The First Seven."
7Wlodkowski, *Motivation and Teaching.*

Inner Child

(You)

When my child cries, throws a fit, and carries on, it's like I lose all my rationality. I want to either scream at them or cave in to their demands to make them stop. I know they're just having a hard time, but I can't bear it! What is wrong with me?!

Help! I'm worried I'm in danger. Expressing these emotions was never safe before. I have to make it stop by any means necessary.

one inner child's point of view

Things to know...

- When you were a child, you did childish things. If you grew up in an environment that wasn't ideal, those childish things might have been met with harm, punishment, hostility, or neglect. **Your brain learned that those behaviors were unsafe.**
- Now that you are grown up, you may know intellectually that those behaviors are part of normal child development. But **your inner child still perceives those behaviors as dangerous.** Out of fear and a natural drive to remain safe, your body and brain begin to act instinctively to try to remove the source of danger.

Things to try...

- **Choose a short script to remind yourself that you are not in danger** when your child acts in a childish way. Write it down, hang it up on your refrigerator, save it to your phone's lock screen—put it anywhere that will help keep it present in your mind. Here are some options that could work:
    - "This is not an emergency." This script meant a lot to me in my first several years of parenting. **Noise immediately made everything feel urgent,** but that was just my own frightened safety response, not a realistic assessment of what was happening.
    - "He's acting four because he's four!" Your brain might jump to expecting your child to react with an adult level of maturity in a stressful situation; **it's easy to forget how few years of experience your child really has.**
    - "It's hard to be four." **This applies forever:** it's also hard to be forty-four.
    - "They're allowed to feel sad." Or mad, or scared, or whatever. **We don't have to talk our kids out of or "fix" their emotions** because emotions are not problems, even when they're uncomfortable.
    - "This isn't about me." It's hard not to take our kids' emotions personally, but usually **they're not directed at us,** even when it feels like they are.
- Try to anticipate which moments are typically difficult for your child, and **take steps to emotionally prepare yourself for their distress.** Sometimes the greatest difficulty for adults lies in the gap between their hopes and expectations. If circumstances are challenging, and you expect your child to melt down but secretly hope they don't, you're now also grappling with your own disappointment when your child does start to struggle. Try to instead get to a place of acceptance. If you can tell yourself something like, "I notice that after school, something always sets her off and she cries for a bit, so that will probably happen today," rather than "I hope she doesn't lose it after school today," her eventual meltdown may not feel as disappointing, sudden, or unsafe for you.

I keep flipping out and screaming at everybody. One minute, I'm telling myself, "It's just noise. They're just playing," and the next, I'm exploding. I don't know why I'm like this.

My sensory system is overwhelmed. I never learned how to figure this stuff out, or what will set me off.

Things to know...

- **Yelling is an intensely self-regulating activity.** It is a big, deep breath; it covers up other, overwhelming sounds; it is a desperate bid for control in an out-of-control situation. It is also damaging to relationships and very hurtful, of course—but you're not just yelling "for no reason." **You are yelling for a reason, and being able to identify that reason will help you find a replacement that isn't so harmful.** Do you need to take a deep breath? Are you unsure of what else to do? Do you need to mute the surrounding noise?
- **Trying to grit your teeth and power through sensory overwhelm on the power of logic and reasoning alone will almost always end in disaster,** because sensory processing is a deeper, more primal process. To put it another way, the more distressed you become, the more of your higher reasoning skills you'll lose access to.

Things to try...

- **Learn about the four sensory processing styles.** If you can identify the patterns in your own sensory processing, you can support yourself by predicting which situations will be tricky much more successfully. (There are lots of written and video resources about sensory processing on my website.[1] There is also a brief explanation of the four styles in the Sensory Processing section of the appendix.)
- **Preemptively use sensory strategies to make yourself feel good throughout the day,** not only when you're already feeling desperate and tapped-out. Maybe you like having something to chew, so you keep gum on hand. Maybe using water to warm up your hands soothes you, so you intentionally wash your hands a few extra times, or slow down the process to appreciate the warm water.
- Identify which less-than-ideal strategies your body reaches for when you're in crisis—yelling, throwing things, swearing, shutting down and ignoring others, fleeing, etc. **Find positive ways to incorporate those activities throughout the day when you're not in crisis.** For example, yell along with your favorite song while you're in the shower, or go for a run early in the morning. These "bad behaviors" can give you powerful clues about what your body finds most regulating, because when your body is in crisis, it will instinctively do whatever will make it feel better. Once you have those clues, you can turn them into strategies. (This is true for children as well as adults!)

I feel like I have to research every single option for my child. I have to ask the opinions of every parent I know. I obsess over what the *one right decision* is. It must exist… it has to, right?

I'm scared that if I make one little mistake, it'll ruin everything. It all depends on me, and I'm not good enough to manage it all perfectly.

Things to know...

- **There is rarely one perfect decision in parenting.** (You probably already know that, but sometimes it helps to have someone tell us things we already know.)
- It is almost impossible to predict how events will progress or make you feel in advance. Making a decision, gaining data from the experience, and adjusting as you go **does not mean that your original decision was a mistake.** It just means that you made the best decision you could with the information you had at the time, and then when you knew more, you made a different decision.
- Having a supportive parent in their corner will make a huge difference to your child. Even if you make all the "right" decisions, your child may end up in a classroom with a teacher who uses methods you don't agree with. They might try out for a sport with a coach who speaks to them more harshly than you're comfortable with, or befriend another child who ends up hurting their relationship, or experience consequences from an authority figure you feel is being unfair. Your child will eventually face tough situations; you can't safeguard them from the entire world. **Your role is to give them a safe place to land when they make a mistake.** You may not be able to protect them from the bumps and bruises of life, but you can protect your relationship with them so they know they are never alone in those emotions.

Things to try...

- **Ask yourself what the genuinely worst outcome of this decision could be.** It might be truly awful for any number of reasons—perhaps the fallout could include a legal hassle, tricky medical complication, or your child hearing messages about themself that are hurtful. **It might also be less awful than you fear**—like a minor administrative headache, a day or two with a changed routine, or a mediocre experience. Either way, being clear about what exactly you're afraid of, rather than constantly rehashing nebulous, undefined anxiety, can help you figure out how much energy to devote to that particular worry and determine the best way forward.
- **Acknowledge your frightened self.** Your fear is doing the best it can to protect you and someone you love deeply. **Thank your fear for doing its best,** take a deep breath, and remind yourself that your fear might not be correct. Practice visualizing your child as capable, even if they encounter a challenging situation, and the two of you as a team that will figure it out together.

She's sitting in my lap again. He's eating food off my plate again. Now they want to crawl into bed with me. I'm sick of it all! I need it to stop! But… don't kids need constant attachment? Am I traumatizing them if I can't be available for them all the time?

This doesn't feel good. I just want some space and to feel like my body belongs to only me. I need for my boundaries to be respected.

Things to know...

- Some adults didn't have healthy levels of touch or affection modeled for them when they were children. **That can make it really hard to figure out how lovey to be with your kids.** It's admirable to want to give your child healthy amounts of cuddles, hugs, and kisses. At the same time, making yourself continually uncomfortable by not honoring your body's boundaries isn't helpful to you!
- The attachment children form with their caregivers is based on a global pattern of warm, connected, loving responses to their needs over months and years of time. **This attachment is not fragile.**[2] Saying no to your child does not disrupt their attachment, and neither does giving your body space from your child's touch sometimes.

Things to try...

- **Practice a few scripted phrases until you feel comfortable saying them warmly and empathetically,** instead of reactively or with frustration.
  - "No thanks, I want some space right now!" **You want your child to be able to say this too** when someone intrudes on their space, such as a peer at school or a sibling who is playing too close. Modeling this for them helps to normalize it.
  - "You can sit next to me if you want." **Suggest to your child what they can do that respects your needs too,** rather than telling them you don't want them on your lap.
  - "I don't like that, please stop." If your child is intentionally getting into your space or pushing past your boundaries, **use clear words with them and move away** or go do something else. (If you only say the words, but do nothing to help your child stop, it doesn't help them understand that it's truly a boundary.)
  - "This is my food. You have some on your plate." Many parents become resentful when it feels like their child is allowed to just take anything of theirs, but they don't feel comfortable stopping them. **This is often rooted in the parent's fear of the child experiencing any uncomfortable emotion**—it may feel easier for the parent to give in than to protect their own boundary and support their child in feeling however they feel about it. But we know that none of our emotions are bad, and none of our emotions need to be fixed. They don't have to be avoided, either, especially at our own expense.

I can't stop worrying about things that I know I can't control. I lay awake at night with my mind racing. I picture every worst-case scenario, and have to bite my tongue to not say "Be careful!" all day long.

What if I don't protect them from everything? What if I can't anticipate every possible problem? What if, what if, what if...? I'm so scared. I need to know that it'll all be okay in the end.

Things to know...

- Anxiety is not just a feeling to simply power through or deal with. **In many cases, anxiety requires professional support.** You are not exaggerating or making up how hard this is. Everybody wants the best for their children, but if you're feeling debilitated by your worries, you might need to explore the support resources you have access to. That could mean talking to a therapist, mentor, support group (whether online or offline), your doctor—whatever is right for you.

- Sometimes, a feeling of desperation for predictability or control comes from a childhood feeling of everything being out of control. Was this something that you struggled with in your childhood? Maybe the home, or homes, you grew up in were chaotic; maybe an important person in your life behaved erratically. Maybe you found your footing by managing every little thing you possibly could. But you were never supposed to have to juggle so many balls: **it was never meant to all be on you.** And other people aren't yours to control, not even for the sake of your own safety. This is a scary, hard thing to work through, and it may take some time. You have done such a good job of looking out for yourself. You deserve a lot of grace.

Things to try...

- **Replace "Be careful" with more meaningful language,** if it's too hard to stop saying it outright. "I see a slippery spot there" and "That branch looks quite high to get down from" both **provide children with helpful, logical information** that a vague "Be careful!" does not.

- **Practice enjoying the small ways in which your children unexpectedly delight you.** You aren't controlling everything they do—and that's a good thing! You could keep a note in your phone of surprising, funny things they say, or intentionally think every night before bed about one spontaneous moment that happened during the day that you're thankful for. Take the time to acknowledge your brain's strong desire to predict as much as possible in order to keep you safe, and to acknowledge that something lovely came out of unpredictability, too. Both are true; it's not an either-or situation.

I don't want to apologize to my child when I snap at them. I don't want to have to constantly connect on only their terms. I don't want to be the one who reaches out every single time. I want things to go my way for once!

I've earned the right to be the one who gets their way. You'll get your turn eventually; right now, it's MINE! I *waited* for this!

one inner child's point of view

Things to know...

- **These types of feelings sometimes come from burnout or exhaustion.** Parenting with grace takes a lot of creativity, and creativity is hard to come by when you're exhausted.
- These feelings are also common if you were raised with "old-school" methods, and **you are trying to do something different now without a lot of resources.** You may feel robbed: you spent your whole childhood waiting for relief from the situation you were in—only to grow up, choose to parent in a different way, and ultimately end up lacking that relief you longed for.

Things to try...

- **Prioritize rest for yourself, whenever and however you can find it.** I know, I know—that is easier said than done. But if you've reached a point where you're resentful of your child for having their emotional needs respected, then both of you desperately need for some of *your* needs to be met, too. Maybe you can find a local teenager who can babysit, or a responsible tween who can play with your child outside or in another room to give you a break now and then. Maybe you can find a new tablet game, a movie, or some art supplies that will keep them occupied for a while so you can spend a few moments relaxing. Maybe you will need to mix and match three different solutions for three kids. If there's anything you can do to prioritize yourself when it feels like no one else will, do it.
- If you don't like playing with your child in a certain way, **offer to connect with them in a different way.** It's completely okay to say "No thanks, I don't want to play with dolls" when it feels like your brain is going to melt out your ears if you have to pretend to be a doll going to school one more time. Your child is allowed to feel sad or wish that you would play, and you are allowed to show them an appropriate way to tell someone that you don't want to do something. (Modeling this helps your child grow up to confidently say no to doing things they don't want to do!) You can suggest a different type of play that you would be comfortable engaging in instead—"I don't want to play with dolls, but I'd love to build a fort out of pillows." Invite them to snuggle on the couch and watch a show with you. Offer to take them outside and draw with chalk together. Whatever feels like it would be bearable (or even enjoyable) to you right now, try bringing your child in on it.
- **Preemptively offer a connecting activity sometimes,** so your child isn't the only one who ever initiates play between you.

the adult's point of view

There's all this talk about how everything is "traumatizing" kids lately. Well, I went through things ten times worse than most kids experience and I turned out fine. I think all this squishy stuff is truly making them too soft.

I had to cope with terrible things at too young of an age. I don't want others to have to cope with what I managed, but I do wish they'd have a little perspective. I wish someone would see how hard it was for me—how hard it still is.

one inner child's point of view

Things to know...

- Three things are true at the same time, here:
  - **The word *trauma* is often overused,** or used by people who don't realize that it has a clinical definition. Adults worry that their actions may be hurting their children emotionally in some way, and use the word *trauma* to describe that hurt.
  - We know more about the brain now than we did fifty years ago, twenty years ago, even ten years ago. **We know more about the long-lasting effects of some harmful ways of treating children,** even ways that have long been considered societally acceptable.
  - You may have experienced some truly traumatizing events as a child. Even if you do not feel traumatized, you may have still gone through some awful things. **Your pain may have never been acknowledged,** and even if you found ways to cope with it and move forward, that pain still lives deep inside you. Sometimes it finds ways to demand that you acknowledge it, if no one else will.

Things to try...

- **Investigate your own feelings, rather than minimizing them.** If something your child does or says upsets you, take a quiet moment later in the day (after the upsetting moment has passed) to reflect on how that felt for you. Some people worry that revisiting uncomfortable or upsetting emotions makes them whiny, negative, or a complainer. But revisiting the moments in which you experienced those emotions, rather than trying to force your body to not feel those emotions, may help you discover what specifically is hard for you.
- Consider whether your child is truly "overreacting" to small things, or if you could in fact be "underreacting" yourself. Your child may be expending their emotional energy immediately in reaction to small disappointments, while you may be saving it all inside—that is, until you can't anymore, and it explodes out of you all at once. Both of these coping mechanisms can be healthy or unhealthy. Bottling your feelings up in an attempt to ignore them forever isn't healthy, but waiting to share how you really feel until you're around a supportive person may be. **Knowing what your strategies are** can help you see them for what they are—strategies for coping with uncomfortable feelings—which, in turn, can help you recognize when your child's strategies may be different than your own, though not necessarily wrong.

the adult's point of view

I didn't know that having children would mean constantly being needed. Not like this. It feels like I'm pouring from a cup that has nothing left in it. I'm doing everything I can to keep smiling, but I'm about to break.

Nobody sees me and all the hard work I do. I take care of everybody else, but nobody takes care of me.

one inner child's point of view

Things to know…

- Some types of childhoods leave adults feeling like the best thing they can do for their children is to continually self-sacrifice. It may help to remember that **you are modeling for your children how to eventually live their own adult lives;** this mindset gives you the freedom to remind yourself that saying things like "No," "I don't want to be climbed on right now," or "My body needs some space" gives your children the language to similarly advocate for themselves.
- **You cannot single-handedly meet 100% of your child's social and emotional needs, and you aren't supposed to.** You can support all of your child's emotions, but children need more than just one person. (There are some circumstances in which this may not be possible for any number of reasons, and in those cases, you may be doing the best possible thing for your child… and yet it's still true that children's needs are greater than any one person can meet alone. Those circumstances are extra-hard *because they are extra-hard*, not because you are failing in any way.)

Things to try…

- "Self-care" has become a buzzword on the internet. **Try to figure out what it means for you personally,** without taking anyone else's opinions into consideration.
  - Do you struggle to **provide yourself with the basics**—eating food at a reasonable time (rather than postponing it to meet someone else's needs), taking medications on a regular basis, drinking enough water? Can you set up reminders on your phone or have a loved one check in with you about these things?
  - Would it help you to **have a dedicated rest time, or access to an activity or hobby that you find restorative?** Can you set up the kids with something special, like a new show, game, or craft material, or a local teenager to baby-sit or tween to play with them in another room while you're still nearby? Can you rearrange your sleep schedule to stay up later or wake up earlier than your children?
  - Can you **use the five senses** to help you identify sensations that feel soothing and revitalizing, so you can give yourself small, yet lovely sensory moments throughout the day? Perhaps you have something you love to taste, something warm or cold to feel in your hands, a favorite scent to breathe in deeply, something soft to pet, a beautiful piece of music to listen to, a fun fidget to fiddle with, a colorful or cherished decoration to hang up somewhere that makes you happy, a phone background you love to look at…

My kids have access to amazing technology. They get to play sports and participate in clubs. When they say they're bored, I just want to take everything away from them and say, "See how you like it!"

I wanted to pursue my dreams and I never got the chance to. Now I've moved heaven and earth to create those opportunities for you. Why won't you appreciate my efforts?

Things to know...

- Kids tend to pick up the definitions of words contextually, rather than by being taught each word's meaning, and **boredom is a tricky emotion to define using contextual clues.** Kids might use the word *bored* to mean that they're anxious about something coming up, or that they want some connection time with their grown-up, or to wish for something specific. Their adult may or may not interpret their complaint accurately, compared to what the child is trying to express.
- Children might not do well in organized sports, or other extracurricular activities with lots of rules to follow, until they are in the tween and teen years. **Sometimes when adults see a child loving a certain type of play, they assume that formalizing it would be even better**—such as signing up a child who loves to experiment with a piano or music-making app for piano lessons, or a child who loves to climb on things and do flips and cartwheels for gymnastics classes. The adult believes they are empowering the child to do what they love. Some children thrive with access to new knowledge and resources like this. For other children, however, **the structured nature of lessons and classes leads them to enjoy the activity much less than when they incorporate it into their own free, child-led play.**

Things to try...

- **Ask yourself whether you are feeling like you missed out on an opportunity in your own childhood.** Did you wish you could have taken dance classes? Did you once love moving your body and wish you could have played a sport? Look into community centers, social clubs, libraries, or other local gathering places and see if there's an activity that you could join! **It's not too late to pursue doing something you love.** If you do, you will even be providing important modeling for your child by engaging with things that delight you. Playing and learning are for all humans, not just for children.
- Children necessarily have a very limited perspective while they are still young. They can't wrap their head around how much an activity costs, how tricky it is to coordinate car rides to practices, and other logistical things like that until they are much older. If you're sacrificing something for your child, it has to be for a reason you believe is important outside of your child appreciating how much you're doing for them. **If you need their gratitude to make it feel worthwhile to you, it might not be a good idea.** Gratitude is a feeling, and we can't force other people to feel certain feelings.

I don't want to hurt my kid the way my parent hurt me, but sometimes when they freak out over nothing, I just want to shake them and say, "This is nothing!"
Why am I like this?

It's not fair. I was never allowed to express my feelings like this. Yes, I want better for you—but it hurts that I never had better for me.

one inner child's point of view

Things to know…

- Empathizing with your child doesn't have to mean that you feel the way they feel, think their feelings are logical, or want them to be reacting that way right then. It's entirely possible to empathetically say, "That's so hard, buddy. I know it's making you sad," without getting dragged down into sadness. All you're doing is acknowledging: **"I have felt deep feelings before, too, at times. I know it is so hard to feel this way."**

Things to try…

- **Give yourself permission to overreact.** This is probably not helpful to do in front of your children, but when you're by yourself, go for it! Get in the car after an extremely boring meeting and yell "UUUUGH!" out loud, paired with your best teenager-style eye roll. When you hear disappointing news, excuse yourself to the bathroom, then stomp your feet and shake your fists. Many of the things toddlers and young children instinctively do with their bodies when they are upset are genuinely helpful self-regulation techniques. Copying them in safe ways may help to discharge some of that negative energy that you may have never learned to channel in other ways.
- **Take steps to make yourself more comfortable while your child is expressing their emotions.** It's okay to wear earplugs or headphones in the house during loud times of day; to play music or predictable TV noise in the background to give your ears something to latch onto; to step away from your sad child to use the toilet, rather than put your needs on hold; and even to continue to move forward with your day, while checking in with your child about where they're at.
- **Both of you are still learning how to live when deeply emotional,** instead of letting your feelings hold you hostage. It takes time to learn this, and trial and error, too. It's okay to make mistakes, apologize for them, and then come back together. You may personally err on the side of "hiding your feelings and cramming them down as far as possible," while your child may err on the side of "spilling their feelings everywhere and splashing them all over everybody," but both of you are going through the same learning process, and on the same team.

the adult's point of view

It feels like my child is the only one who behaves so
badly… like I'm the only one who can't keep up with
everything—managing the house, work, the kids…
it feels like I'm failing.

I don't know how to handle all of this. Nobody ever
showed me how or prepared me for it. I'm scared people
will see that I'm just guessing at how to do this right…
I can't let them see.

one inner child's point of view

Things to know...

- **Parenting is hard, in some capacity, for absolutely every parent.** You are not failing because parenting feels hard; you are a human who is doing a hard thing, and that is why the thing feels hard.

- The demands of today's world make it really hard to do everything. **Family units are expected to carry a lot of burdens in isolation** that might have been shared among larger, more interconnected communities in the past. Managing a house is a full-time job, parenting is a full-time job, and of course, working at a full-time job is a full-time job. Whether you are doing only one of these things or a few at a time, or these things plus something else (like enjoying a hobby, volunteering, or traveling), the time adds up quickly. It feels overwhelming because it is.

- Huge, global, stressful events are happening around us all the time, and there are a lot of ways in which that stress is dumped directly into our minds pretty much 24/7. **Many people, children included, are living in constantly stressed-out bodies,** because they are carrying the weight of all that stress on top of trying to survive the day-to-day routine.

- Many people who were raised in a less-than-ideal environment come away from that experience with a **fear of being caught making a mistake.** If making a mistake was met with punishment, ridicule, or belittlement when you were a child, you might feel constant pressure now to juggle everything at once, because it would be overwhelmingly scary for anyone else to see you drop a single ball.

Things to try...

- If possible, **identify a friend, family member, or other loved one with whom you can be honest about how you are feeling.** It might help if you can text someone you trust, "Today is going really badly because..." and receive a response that feels genuinely supportive. Humans are made for community; **having someone who you feel is on your side and who you don't fear judgment from can go a long way.**

- **Acknowledge your own scared inner child.** When life feels overwhelming and you feel like you're failing, notice your thought process. What sorts of things does your brain say to you when you're overwhelmed? Can you empathize with your brain as if it were a toddler melting down, without berating it for melting down in the first place? "Whew, I must be feeling so scared. I can tell because my heart is racing. Well, I'm not in danger right now. This is really hard, and I can survive it."

Key themes from this work:

1. **It's hard to see our children take for granted something we wish we'd had.** Whether that's an actual object, an experience, or a feeling of emotional safety, sometimes watching our children treat something precious as if it's mundane can pick at a sore place inside of us. It's ironic, too, because that's literally a metric for success. We have provided our children with protection from the hurt we felt: now they don't understand, on an emotional level, how that hurt affected us. It feels hard because it *is* hard. We can both own that and acknowledge that the emotional difficulty isn't our children's fault—their blissful ignorance of our pain is a good thing.

2. Children often have a knack for mirroring things in ourselves that we have strong feelings about. They're quirky in ways that we, ourselves, were made fun of for. They're loud and unabashed in ways that we, ourselves, were told to quiet down for. Their emotions spill out in ways that we were expected to squash. They look us in the eye and unknowingly challenge us, **because to accept them the way they are is to acknowledge that what was done to our younger selves was wrong.**

3. **The patterns that were modeled for each of us in childhood have grown deep roots.** It takes hard, intentional work to do something different than the "default" your brain learned. Whether the parenting you experienced was something you admire and emulate or never want to carry on was completely a matter of chance. You didn't choose how you were raised, and you didn't create those defaults in your brain, so they don't say anything about you. It's incredibly powerful and brave to choose to change them. Many people never do.

4. Almost all of us have a hard time with some aspect of parenting. Maybe it's the worry or the uncertainty. Maybe it's the inability to control what another person chooses to do. Maybe it's the sensory, emotional, mental, or physical overwhelm. Maybe it's coping with an unexpected disability. Maybe becoming a parent wasn't a decision, but something that just happened to you. Maybe it's grieving the loss of someone who you thought would be a part of your parenting journey. Maybe it's shaking off old patterns and creating something new. Maybe it's navigating a trauma. **In some way, every single one of us has a hard time with parenting.**

Parenting is a hard thing to do. And reparenting yourself alongside that? Looking at your own little self and loving them, even if no one else did? That may be the hardest thing you'll ever do. **And I'm so, so proud of you for doing it.**

Notes

1Olds, "The Occuplaytional Therapist."
2Peluso et al., "Comparison of Attachment Theory."

Acknowledgements

If I tried to write out the names of everyone who has encouraged me along my writing journey, it would double the length of this book, because the truth is that everyone who has ever participated in my online community has been a part of my writing this book. Every day on my page, "The Occuplaytional Therapist," I get to discuss ideas, polish my writing, and refine my beliefs with an enthusiastic crowd of like-minded people. These interactions have shaped me as a person, as a therapist, and as a parent. I am grateful for this community every single day.

There are some people who I want to thank more specifically. My Shipwrecked friends—Kat Parys, Kit Ward-Crixell, Evan Compton, Charlie Murphy, Mike Cossairt, and Billy Morgan—for, alternately, writing with me and delightfully distracting me from writing.

Pyper Dee, Amy Lynn, Jennifer Singleton, Lauren Williams, and Linda Voelkel, who were so loudly supportive of my work online that you became the first ones to see any part of this book and give me suggestions for how to make it better. Sarah Lauterbach, Kindree Mieling, Samantha MacMillan, Missy Carvin, Rebekah Nicodemus, Laura Ritter, Natalia Earley, Heather Corby, Jess Gavin, Nora Bryan, Annemieke Oosterling, Lindsay Guy-Decker, Maria Vander Meulen, Pauline Chambers, Samantha Jannenga Hanks, and Erin Kardolus, who further looked through and helped me refine many of its pages. Guy Stephens, Cass Griffin Bennett, Suzanne Axelsson, Autball, and Suzi Mohn, thank you for your willingness to put your names behind my work, as well as your private words of encouragement and support.

All the friends I've made through my work online, including Lachy Rowe, Denita Dinger, Elizabeth Jarvis, Alex Watson, Shubha Bala, and so many more. Whether we talked about this book specifically or not, your friendship and encouragement have kept me writing.

The stellar cover art comes from the incredibly talented Courtney Herwicz, who took my scattered rambles about what this book was about and turned them into the perfect design.

Kristina Hawley, my amazing editor, I am exceptionally grateful that you agreed to work with me. You pushed this book to be better in so many ways and brought invaluable expertise to the project. It wouldn't have become what it is without you.

My first and forever fan club, Shea Harrell, Erica Falconbury, and Kim Gutierrez. Amy Watson, Ms. DABA (I can't call you anything other than Ms. DABA, sorry), and everyone else at Feltwell and Lakenheath Elementary Schools, where I grew into the therapist I am today. My explaining children's confusing behaviors in hundreds of

IEP meetings fueled my ability to write coherently about them, and vice versa. It was an honor to work alongside you all. I still can't believe you made T-shirts.

My dearest Rachel Landers. You are beloved and adored by my entire family; you give me a window into the future, into what parenting big kids looks like; you make me feel like the best version of myself. And you can successfully put my children to bed, which is the pinnacle of human achievement.

Everybody who was a part of my time at EDIS, especially Laura Dossett, Jonathan Topham, Francesca Culp, Chad Killpack, Linda Felini-Smith, Renee Hoover, Matt Scott, and Kimberly Dorsett. You were the best team anyone could've asked for.

The absolutely irreplaceable Maddie Compton, whose friendship is near-impossible to describe in a single word. Coworker? Officemate? Friend? None of these come close to touching what you are to me. You have probably had eight books' worth of content rambled in your direction, only some of which you asked for. I send you all my gratitude, thoughts, encouragement, and a water break.

My children, whose take-the-world-by-storm, beautiful, joyful, tenacious, self-confident incomprehensibility pushes me every day to forget what I think I know and discover new ways of living, doing, and being. I love you both with all my heart.

And the magnificent Dr. Josh Olds, the best dad I know. I have loved you for so long that it is just a fact of life now, encoded into my DNA, a constant of our physical universe. I would go anywhere with you.

Appendix

Executive Functioning

Lots of subskills fall under the header of executive functioning, and these complicated skills essentially work together to pilot the brain:

- Attention controls which information the brain is taking in versus filtering out at any given time.

- Impulse control monitors the action impulses that arise in the brain and decides which to carry out and which to ignore.

- Planning involves predicting the future and trying to act in a way that will yield the result you want.

- Memory skills are how the brain holds onto information long enough to decide what to do with it. They can be further divided into the types of skills where the memory is revisited right away, like working memory and short-term memory, or where the memory is pulled from a long time ago, like implicit and explicit long-term memory.

Executive functioning starts in infancy, with the development of attention.[1] It continues to grow throughout childhood and beyond, into the teenage and even adult years. Many adults mistakenly expect children to have certain executive functioning skills a very long time before their bodies actually begin to develop those skills. For example, our brains don't begin to know how to reject certain impulses until we are between three and five years old.[2] Even once that skill has developed, emotional or exciting circumstances make it harder to control impulses. Despite that, adults interpret two-year-olds' impulsivity as defiance so commonly that our society has the stereotype of the "terrible twos."

Before children have a certain executive functioning skill, and while they are in the process of developing it, they need adult support. In this capacity, the adult is functioning as an external, wiser, more developed brain on behalf of the child's brain. Here are some ways in which an adult could do this:

- Supportively direct the child's attention—"Look over here!" or "Listen up, guys!"

- Patiently interrupt the child's impulsive motor plan (see the following section for more about motor plans).

- Prompt the child's memory: "Do you remember what you need before we can go to the park? (pause) They go on your feet…?"

- Show the child how to plan, either with tools or by talking out loud. "Okay, what materials will you need for this project? Let's think it through and I'll write them down."

Interoception

The word *interoception* can basically be defined as your "inner body sense." Interoception involves being aware of and interpreting the physical sensations that occur inside your body. These can be emotional, like recognizing that tears are stinging the back of your eyes because you are sad. They can be biological, like being able to tell that a burning, tingling, full sensation in your bladder means that you need to use the toilet.

Interoception is also very personal. One person's interpretation of the physical sensation "My hands are hot and sweaty" could be that they are feeling anxious, while another person's interpretation of that same sensation could be that they need to take their jacket off, and both could be correct about their own bodies.

Kelly Mahler, another occupational therapist, is the leading expert on interoception and has created many resources about it. These are freely available on her website as well as offered in the form of books like *The Interoception Curriculum: A Step-by-Step Guide to Developing Mindful Self-Regulation.*[3] Another interoceptive resource I love, this one for its child-friendliness, is *The Galaxy Guide to Running My Rocket* by Ready Rocket Resources.[4]

Motor Planning

Throughout the book, I sometimes refer to motor planning as *action planning*, because that's the simplest way to conceptualize it. Here, the word *motor* means "movement." *Motor planning* refers to the way that brains carry out a movement or physical action.

The brain is made up of cells called neurons. One neuron will activate, causing the neuron it's touching to activate, which causes the neuron that one is touching to activate, and so on, to create a pathway. This chain of activation moving along a pathway—specifically, one of the pathways that connects to the nerves that control our muscles—is what leads to a physical action.

When a brain causes an action to happen for the very first time, the movements are clumsy, uncertain, or weak. Think of how a baby first learns to move their whole arm by flinging it across their body. Over time, that pathway is used repeatedly, and new neurons along the pathway are activated as the pathway is pruned and refined. The baby learns to move only their elbow or wrist, or to open and close their fingers to pick up something they want to grab.

The more a motor plan is practiced, the stronger it becomes. This is sometimes called *muscle memory*; maybe you have experienced it. I once worked at a job where I had to enter a seven-digit PIN into a keypad in order to access the workplace. If I was asked to verbally recite the number, I would have to really think about it—but if I stood in front of a keypad and simply let my hand move, I could enter it immediately. My brain's neurons have activated in exactly that order so many times that the movement has become a strong motor plan.

This is relevant when we want to stop children from doing a specific action, or redirect them into a new, more constructive action. One example of this is that adults may let a small child hit them over and over, and simply ignore the blows because the child is small and isn't using enough force for it to hurt. The adults may try to verbally redirect the child, perhaps by saying "Don't hit" or "We don't use hands for hitting," in an attempt to be gentle and positive in their caregiving.

This is admirable. The only problem is that the child is still solidifying and practicing the motor plan. Their body and brain are strengthening the sensorimotor sequence of events: "When I am mad, this neuron activates, which activates that one, then that one… and then I hit." As the child grows bigger, their hits become stronger and more targeted, because they have been practicing that motor plan over and over.

This is why blocking the motor plan is an important part of redirection. This can take the form of steering the motor plan toward a new target (such as "You can hit this pillow"), interrupting the motor plan (such as the adult placing their hand on the child's fist and physically stopping it from moving or connecting with another part of their body), or a combination of both (like blocking the child's hand while retrieving a pillow, then handing them the pillow to hit).

It takes time to learn a new motor plan, especially if it's associated with a strong emotion, like anger and hitting. It won't happen after just one or two redirections, but with patient repetition, time, and maturity, brains do start to create new motor plans.

Proprioception

I usually define the word *proprioception* as "deep body sense." Think of the difference between someone touching you lightly on the shoulder versus squeezing your shoulder. The former is a part of the touch (tactile) system, and the latter—involving a squeeze—is proprioception. You feel it deep in your body rather than on your skin. When you tense your bicep and hold that tension, you feel a sensation deep in your arm that is kind of like a squeeze from somebody else. That internally tensed feeling is also your proprioception.

The "sensing" part of it also has to do with your sense of where your body is in space, in relation to both your body itself and other objects. People who have a poor sense of proprioception tend to be clumsier; they are less aware of their body's position in space compared to other objects or people.

Proprioception is sometimes called the "universal regulator" in that nearly everybody finds proprioceptive input to be regulating for their body in some way. This means it can be really powerful to know a little bit about proprioception, because finding quick shortcuts to getting proprioceptive input can help both you and your child regulate your emotions more quickly.

I divide proprioception into three subcategories: exertion, impact, and pressure.

Exertion comes from using muscles—pushing, pulling, lifting something heavy, climbing, hanging from something, tensing your muscles—all these activities provide exertion and proprioceptive input. Some playful ways to seek out exertion could be to race through an obstacle course, throw a ball or Frisbee, or hang from a chin-up bar. You can incorporate elements of self-competition into these (like trying to beat a timed record) or blend them with kids' interests (like pretending to throw a Poké Ball to catch a Pokémon).

Impact comes from the body, or part of the body, colliding with something else. Clapping provides impact: one hand hits the other. Jumping provides impact: both feet hit the ground. Wrestling, falling, running, hitting, kicking, rolling, and banging all provide impact and proprioceptive input. One of the fastest ways to seek out impact is to roughhouse, but if that's not available or not appropriate (for example, in a school setting), there are other ways to playfully get impact feedback. Many sports involve kicking or hitting a ball around; many types of percussion instruments provide impact feedback through the hands (think of hitting the keys on a marimba or the head of a drum). Many playground games involve jumping, including hopscotch, jump rope, and the childhood classic of pretending the ground is lava.

Pressure comes from squeezing or weight. Putting something heavy on yourself, like a weighted blanket, a pet, or a pile of stuffed animals, provides pressure. Getting a tight hug from someone you love provides pressure. Cocooning yourself in blankets and sitting on the couch provides pressure. Draping yourself over furniture and putting more of your body in contact with surfaces (like lying down versus standing up) both provide pressure. Pressure is often a slow-motion sensory input, so it can be harder to incorporate into play, but the cuddly, cozy nature of it lends itself well to moments of connection, even if they're not high-energy.

When someone is feeling unsettled, whether that's from sadness, anger, impatience, anxiety, excitement, silliness, or something else, getting more proprioceptive input is one good way to help. Trying out the different kinds of proprioception, while paying attention to what feels especially good in your body, is a good place to start.

Schema Play

Play schemas can be thought of as phases of play that many children go through. Schemas do not have to be taught; they are more like observations about common stages of play development.

Knowing about play schemas can help adults be more understanding when their child is gravitating toward the same baffling or annoying actions over and over. Play schemas are very common in the toddler and preschool years, as children are basically tiny scientists exploring the physical properties of the world through extensive, repeated research. Some examples of play schemas include:

- Trajectory schema—throwing things, watching them fly through the air, predicting how and where they will land, contemplating all the sensory minutiae that goes along with a landing. What sound will it make? How will it bounce? Who will react and how?

- Connection schema—putting things together in "correct" and "incorrect" ways. How do things attach? How solid are those attachments? This often includes disconnecting things, too, which can sometimes look like "destroying things" or "being aggressive."

- Rotation schema—rolling, spinning, twirling. This is closely linked with the body's *vestibular* sense, which is how the inner ear provides balance and creates dizziness when it is disrupted.

- Orientation schema—looking at things from different angles. This may involve everything from turning over objects to look at their undersides, to crawling beneath tables, to hanging upside-down.

- Enclosing schema—putting things inside all kinds of different containers (as well as spilling their contents back out again).

- Transporting schema—moving things from one place to another, carrying things around with them at all times. (The TV remote may end up in the bathroom and the toothbrush may end up in the playroom!)

There are many other potential types of play schemas, too. These definitions were all taken from the book *Understanding Schemas in Young Children;* [5] other sources may provide additional schema definitions.

If a particular type of play action that a child is gravitating toward needs to be replaced or redirected, choosing one that falls within the same schema can make the redirection much more successful. For example, if a child is constantly throwing heavy toys across the room, perhaps endangering others or damaging the walls, then the child needs easy access to lots of soft things that can be playfully thrown to their heart's content.

Sensory Processing

Every human has ways of processing the sensory input they take in from the world around them. You may have learned about the five senses: sight, hearing, smell, taste, and touch. There are other senses, too, like proprioception (defined previously in this appendix). As the brain gets sensory information from all the sense organs—the eyes, ears, nose, tongue, and skin—it has to process that information and then do something with it.

There is way more information in our surroundings than our brains can take in at any given time. There may be hundreds of tiny, individual visual details in your surroundings, for example, and your brain can't pay rapt attention to every single one of them. So, your brain filters out what it thinks it doesn't need and focuses on what it thinks it does need. It usually focuses on either things of importance and value to you, or things that pose a threat or a danger to you, because your brain wants to protect you and pursue your goals.

Some people's "filters" get overwhelmed quickly. These people may seek out quiet environments, because the strain of filtering out all the noise in a noisy environment uses up too much of their brain's energy for the day. (They may also get overwhelmed by sights, tastes, smells, or any other type of sense—not just hearing.)

Other people don't get overwhelmed in that way. In fact, they may actually need more (or stronger) sensory input for their brain to even pick up on it—for it to meet their threshold for what they can pay attention to, because everything weaker than that is getting filtered out completely. These people may seek out more noise, brighter colors, flashier lights, more movement, etc., because these types of input help their body feel alert, settled, and capable.

Sensory processing styles are morally neutral. Each style has its own positives and negatives, and is simply a part of the beautiful diversity in the human race. Knowing the differences between the sensory processing styles helps to identify when there is an actual physical need for more or less sensory input that the body is trying to meet. Actions related to sensory processing are very commonly misunderstood or misinterpreted as "bad behavior," and understanding why people may move toward or away from sources of sensory input can help us more accurately assess those types of situations.

Notes

[1]Blankenship et al., "Attention and Executive Functioning."

[2]Best and Miller, "A Developmental Perspective."

[3]Mahler, *The Interoception Curriculum.*

[4]Ready Rocket Resources, *The Galaxy Guide.*

[5]Louis et al., *Understanding Schemas.*

Bibliography

Ames, Louise Bates, and Frances L Ilg. *Your Six-Year-Old: Loving and Defiant.* New York: Dell, 1981.

Best, John R., and Patricia H. Miller. "A Developmental Perspective on Executive Function." *Child Development* 81, no. 6 (November/December 2010): 1641–60. https://doi.org/10.1111/j.1467-8624.2010.01499.x.

Blankenship, Tashauna L., Madeline A. Slough, Susan D. Calkins, Kirby Deater-Deckard, Jungmeen Kim-Spoon, and Martha Ann Bell. "Attention and Executive Functioning in Infancy: Links to Childhood Executive Function and Reading Achievement." *Developmental Science* 22, no. 6 (November 2019): e12824. https://doi.org/10.1111/desc.12824.

CDC. "Important Milestones: Your Child By Eighteen Months." CDC's Developmental Milestones. Last reviewed June 6, 2023. https://www.cdc.gov/ncbddd/actearly/milestones/milestones-18mo.html.

Center for Parenting Education, The. "Child Development by Age." Accessed June 6, 2024. https://centerforparentingeducation.org/library-of-articles/child-development/child-development-by-age/

Checkley, Kathy. "The First Seven… And the Eighth: A Conversation with Howard Gardner." *Educational Leadership* 55, no. 1 (September 1997): 8–13. https://eric.ed.gov/?id=EJ550524.

Cohen, Lawrence J. *Playful Parenting: An Exciting New Approach to Raising Children That Will Help You Nurture Closer Connections, Solve Behavior Problems, and Encourage Confidence.* New York: Ballantine Books, 2002.

Cole, Natasha Chong, Ruopeng An, Soo-Yeun Lee, and Sharon M. Donovan. "Correlates of Picky Eating and Food Neophobia in Young Children: A Systematic Review and Meta-Analysis." *Nutrition Reviews* 75, no. 7 (July 2017): 516–32. https://doi.org/10.1093/nutrit/nux024.

Cools, Roshan, Monja Fröbose, Esther Aarts, and Lieke Hofmans. "Dopamine and the Motivation of Cognitive Control." *Handbook of Clinical Neurology* 163 (2019): 123–43. https://doi.org/10.1016/B978-0-12-804281-6.00007-0.

Delahooke, Mona. *Brain-Body Parenting: How to Stop Managing Behavior and Start Raising Joyful, Resilient Kids.* New York: Harper, 2022.

Diekman, Amanda. *Low-Demand Parenting: Dropping Demands, Restoring Calm, and Finding Connection with Your Uniquely Wired Child.* Philadelphia: Jessica Kingsley Publishers, 2023.

Einzig, Robin. "It's All My Fault. All of It." *Visible Child* (blog). July 28, 2015. https://visiblechild.com/2015/07/28/ its-all-my-fault-all-of-it/.

Engle, Randall W., Julie J. Carullo, and Kathryn W. Collins. "Individual Differences in Working Memory for Comprehension and Following Directions." *The Journal of Educational Research* 84, no. 5 (1991): 253–62. https:// doi.org/10.1080/00220671.1991.10886025.

Erikson, Erik H. *Childhood and Society.* New York: W. W. Norton & Company, 1993. First published 1950.

Faber, Adele, and Elaine Mazlish. *How to Talk So Kids Will Listen & Listen So Kids Will Talk.* New York: Scribner, 2022. First published 2012.

Greene, Ross W. *Lost at School: Why Our Kids with Behavioral Challenges Are Falling Through the Cracks and How We Can Help Them.* New York: Scribner, 2014. First published 2008.

Greene, Ross W. *Raising Human Beings: Creating a Collaborative Partnership with Your Child.* New York: Scribner, 2016.

Hanscom, Angela J. *Balanced and Barefoot: How Unrestricted Outdoor Play Makes for Strong, Confident, and Capable Children.* Oakland: New Harbinger Publications, 2016.

Hughes, Bob. *A Playworker's Taxonomy of Play Types.* London: Playlink, 2002. First published 1996.

Ivanova, E. F. "The Development of Voluntary Behavior in Preschoolers: Repetition of Z. V. Manuilenko's Experiments." *Journal of Russian and East European Psychology* 38, no. 2 (2000): 6–21. https://doi.org/10.2753/ rpo1061-040538026.

Jummani, Rahil R., and Jess P. Shatkin. "Phamacological Interventions." In *Handbook of Cognitive Behavioral Therapy for Pediatric Medical Conditions*, edited by Robert D. Friedberg and Jennifer K. Paternostro, 151–169. Cham: Springer, 2019. https://doi.org/10.1007/978-3-030-21683-2_11.

Lansbury, Janet. *No Bad Kids: Toddler Discipline Without Shame.* JLML Press, 2014.

Louis, Stella, Clare Beswick, Liz Magraw, and Lisa Hayes. *Understanding Schemas in Young Children: Again! Again!* London: Featherstone, 2018. First published 2008 as *Again! Again!*.

"Magic ToDo," GoblinTools, accessed June 6, 2024, https://goblin.tools.

Mahler, Kelly. *The Interoception Curriculum: A Step-By-Step Framework for Developing Mindful Self-Regulation.* Hershey: Kelly Mahler, 2019.

Milligan, Karen, Janet Wilde Astington, and Lisa Ain Dack. "Language and Theory of Mind: Meta-Analysis of the Relation Between Language Ability and False-Belief Understanding." *Child Development* 78, no. 2 (March–April 2007): 622–46. https://doi.org/10.1111/j.1467-8624.2007.01018.x.

Molineux, Matthew. *A Dictionary of Occupational Science and Occupational Therapy*: Oxford: Oxford University Press, 2017. http://dx.doi.org/10.1093/acref/9780191773624.001.0001.

Nucci, Larry P. "The Development of Moral Reasoning." In *Blackwell Handbook of Childhood Cognitive Development*, edited by Usha Goswami, 303–325. Oxford: Blackwell, 2002. https://doi.org/10.1002/9780470996652.ch14.

Olds, Kelsie. "The Occuplaytional Therapist," The Occuplaytional Therapist, accessed June 6, 2024, https://www.occuplaytional.com.

Peluso, Paul R., Jennifer P. Peluso, JoAnna F. White, and Roy M. Kern. "A Comparison of Attachment Theory and Individual Psychology: A Review of the Literature." *Journal of Counseling & Development* 82, no. 2 (2004): 139–45. https://doi.org/10.1002/j.1556-6678.2004.tb00295.x.

Ready Rocket Resources. *The Galaxy Guide to Running My Rocket*. Perth: Ready Rocket Resources, 2023.

Rubin, Kenneth H. "Egocentrism in Childhood: A Unitary Construct?" *Child Development* 44, no. 1 (March 1973): 102–10. https://doi.org/10.2307/1127685.

Shanker, Stuart. *Self-Reg: How to Help Your Child (and You) Break the Stress Cycle and Successfully Engage with Life*. London: Penguin Books, 2017.

Sharon, Tanya, and Jacqueline D. Woolley. "Do Monsters Dream? Young Children's Understanding of the Fantasy/Reality Distinction." *British Journal of Developmental Psychology* 22, no. 2 (June 2004): 293–310. https://doi.org/10.1348/026151004323044627.

Wise, Roy A. "Dopamine, Learning and Motivation." *Nature Reviews Neuroscience* 5 (2004): 483–94. https://doi.org/10.1038/nrn1406.

Wlodkowski, Raymond J. *Motivation and Teaching: A Practical Guide*. Washington, DC: National Education Association, 1986.

Wolfson, Amy R., and Mary A. Carskadon. "Sleep Schedules and Daytime Functioning in Adolescents." *Child Development* 69, no. 4 (August 1998): 875–87. https://doi.org/10.2307/1132351.

Made in the USA
Middletown, DE
12 September 2024

60833841R10102